PARIS CHIC & TRENDY
DESIGNERS' Studios • HIP Boutiques • VINTAGE Shops

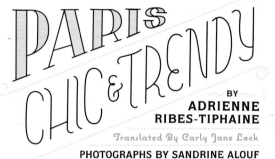

PARIS CHIC & TRENDY

BY
**ADRIENNE
RIBES-TIPHAINE**

Translated By Carly Jane Lock

PHOTOGRAPHS BY SANDRINE ALOUF

DESIGNERS' Studios

~

HIP Boutiques

~

VINTAGE Shops

THE LITTLE BOOKROOM · NEW YORK

Originally published as *Paris Chic & Trendy • Ateliers de créateurs, boutiques branches, répaires vintage*
© Editions Parigramme, Paris, France, 2006 • © Adrienne Ribes-Tiphaine • Photos © Sandrine Alouf

Book Design: Louise Fili Ltd

Printed in China

Library of Congress Cataloging-in-Publication
Ribes-Tiphaine, Adrienne.
[Paris chic & trendy. English]
Paris chic and trendy : designers' studios, hip boutiques, vintage shops
Adrienne Ribes-Tiphaine; photos by Sandrine Alouf;
translated by Carly Jane Lock.
p. cm.
Includes index.
ISBN 1-892145-53-7
1. Shopping—France—Paris—Guidebooks. 2. Clothing trade—
France—Paris—Guidebooks. 3. Paris (France)—Guidebooks. I. Title.
TX337.F82P378713 2008
381'.4564130244361--dc22
2007020778

Published by The Little Bookroom
1755 Broadway, 5th floor
New York NY 10019
www.littlebookroom.com
(212) 293-1643 Fax (212) 333-5374
editorial@littlebookroom.com

1 3 5 7 9 10 8 6 4 2

Distributed in the United States by Random House and in the UK by Signature Book Services.

FOR MY TWIN GIRLS
"My Two Bright Stars" born in 2005.

~

for PARISIAN WOMEN and for the MEN and WOMEN WHO
BRING CHIC to the STREETS and MAKE LIFE BEAUTIFUL.
R.-T.

~

for ROMANE CRUZ, a future chic Parisian woman.

~

thanks to
SANDRINE, LESLIE, FLORENCE, AURÉTIE, CHARLOTTE,
my dear Parisian friends.
S. A.

CONTENTS

INTRODUCTION

A certain allure, indefinable chic, audacity down to a T, a real eye for trends, femininity captured with grace, freedom of spirit...When it comes to defining the Parisian woman or incarnating her on screen, these are the features that define her. It's an age-old combination that has made Paris a hotbed of trends, a place where fashion lives through those who create and adorn it.

In Paris, fashion comes naturally. Its catwalk shows are the most popular in the world, and Parisian designers export their wares from New York to Tokyo—scoffing all the while at trends with invincible tenacity. Top bag and shoe designers, discreet atelier queens, multi-brand stores that bring clothes together like DJs in the mix, the fantastically busy bees of vintage chic...You'll find them all here, passionate and determined to stand up for their own fashion at all costs, with styles sometimes so different yet always complementary. Sampling, recapturing, and reinterpreting: in Paris, there is "independent designer fashion" just like there is "independent film." This fashion, unique to Parisian women, which by prohibiting uniformity, enables each woman to express her personality and innermost self. It is not by chance that this book honors many adopted Parisians who hail, for example, from the banks of the Bosphorus or California, since Paris remains a meeting point for couture designers, a city that still sees lovers flock to its elegant riverbanks.

From the fifty-four featured Parisian hotspots, a secret itinerary unravels before our eyes spanning the "fashion bastion" ateliers of the Bastille area, rue St-Honoré, the heights of Montmartre, and over to the Left Bank's emblematic shopping arteries, which together make Paris what it has never ceased to be: The all-time moving and shaking capital of fashion.

La mode de Paris fait d'une
femme une récompense.

Paris fashion makes being a woman worthwhile.

~

LOUISE DE VILMORIN

AGNÈS B.

6, rue DU JOUR, 1ST ARR.
Téléphone: 01 45 08 56 56 • Metro: LES HALLES
MONDAY to SATURDAY 10am–7pm (7:30pm in the summer)
www.agnesb.fr • SEE P. 174 FOR OTHER BOUTIQUES

If there were such a thing as the "Académie française of fashion," Agnès B. would be its perpetual director. The former pupil of the École des Beaux-Arts in Versailles, née Agnès Troublé (who married editor Christian Bourgois, hence the "B" of her trade name), debuted as fashion editor for *Elle* magazine. Two years at Dorothée Bis (1964–1966) taught her the tricks of the stylist trade, then ten years later at thirty-four, after training with different labels (V de V, Limitex, Pierre d'Alby), she opened her first womenswear boutique on rue du Jour in an old butcher shop. While

keeping the original white tiling and black-boards, the designer enriched and personalized the boutique with a collage of torn posters and postcards, with the latest rock tunes playing over and over again for background music. On the clothes racks: worker's dungarees and jackets (re-shaped and dyed), cotton painter's pants, gauzy skirts—all garments that would later become her basics or signature pieces. Bestsellers included the striped sailor's T-shirt, the snap cardigan with mother-of-pearl fastenings, the white poplin shirt, a double-breasted Manet-inspired fife player's jacket. Her classics are often very chic with some audacious pieces,

despite sticking to the same fabrics. The brand's international success has not faltered since it was founded in 1975 (the rerelease of the super-famous cardigan, revisited and newly restructured at the waist, is still Agnès B.'s best-selling item), nor has the designer's vocation as head of the house dwindled either. Her clothes are often mouthpieces for major charitable causes; she invites famous and unknown contemporary artists as guest designers, or publicizes causes in her own publications and exhibitions held at the designer's excellent art gallery on rue Quincampoix. Choosing Agnès B. is about preferring lasting happiness to the passing fancy.

AMERICAN APPAREL

31, place du MARCHÉ-SAINT-HONORÉ, 1ST ARR.
Telephone: 01 42 60 03 72 • Metro: PYRAMIDES
MONDAY to SATURDAY 10:30am – 7:30pm
SEE P. 174 FOR OTHER BOUTIQUES • www.americanapparel.net

S tand corrected: a T-shirt is not a mere basic! Thousands of examples that prove it can be found at American Apparel, where you won't go away without feeling overwhelmed by the number of variations of the quin-T-essential garment. They come in every imaginable shape and form: V-neck, stand-up collar, puffed or three-quarter sleeves, slightly fitted or loose, XXL or XS. A word of advice? Forget black or white—there are more than forty colors to choose from on the racks. This stateside brand star, renowned for its cool and sexy connotations, became a favorite with Parisian women after opening its first store in 2004. An immediate hit—American Apparel, with organic cotton onesies (for *au naturel* tiny tots), how-low-can-you-go hipster boxer shorts (for the teenage market), bra-and-knickers sets, sweatshirts, petticoats, and other bedroom attire, made its way into the closets and underwear drawers of the capital's most demanding dressers. You can't fault the cotton's excellent quality, the way the garments keep their shape, and the no-logo policy—

something of a rarity today—all at very reasonable prices and made in downtown L.A. In these fair-trade-conscious times, we must not forget that American Apparel, founded in Los Angeles in 1997 by Dov Charney, a charismatic libertarian forty-something, is a company that pays its employees well, gives them social security coverage, recycles tons of scrap fabric, and fights against outsourcing to Asia. Clothes save America!

ANTIK BATIK

4, rue CAMBON, 1ST ARR.
Telephone: 01 40 15 01 45 • Metro: CONCORDE
MONDAY to SATURDAY 10:30am–7pm
SEE P. 174 FOR OTHER BOUTIQUE • www.antikbatik.fr

Don't even think of setting foot in an Antik Batik shop without your passport! This brand's Paris ports-of-call beckon you to journey to Bombay, Marrakesh, Rio de Janeiro, and everywhere in between. A far cry from the Brazilian charm bracelets that were brought back to Paris in 1992 as a first shot at introducing ethnic fashion, in the space of a few years Antik Batik became the capital's most-sought-after exotic-chic fashion brand. Its recipe for success: a series of wraps in original colors designed and made in Bali by masters of the ancestral wax-printing art. Since then, Antik Batik has made no secret of their creed that honors the world's best craftsmanship with small lines of handmade pieces loved by the likes of Vanessa Paradis, Monica Bellucci, and also Julia Roberts and Uma Thurman, who have all donned one of the sexy kurtas (those traditional collarless Indian tunics with three buttons).

Other offerings include low-cut tunics slashed to mid thigh, delicate Tuareg tattoo-print T-shirts, beaded tops, and dresses embroidered with multicolored sequins, all made of fluid, sexy, sheer fabrics: silk and cotton voile in summer, velvet and cashmere in winter. Colors from around the world are applied to accessories, fine lingerie, and a children's range. This is fashion without frontiers for urban women who are fed up with the dreary gray of concrete.

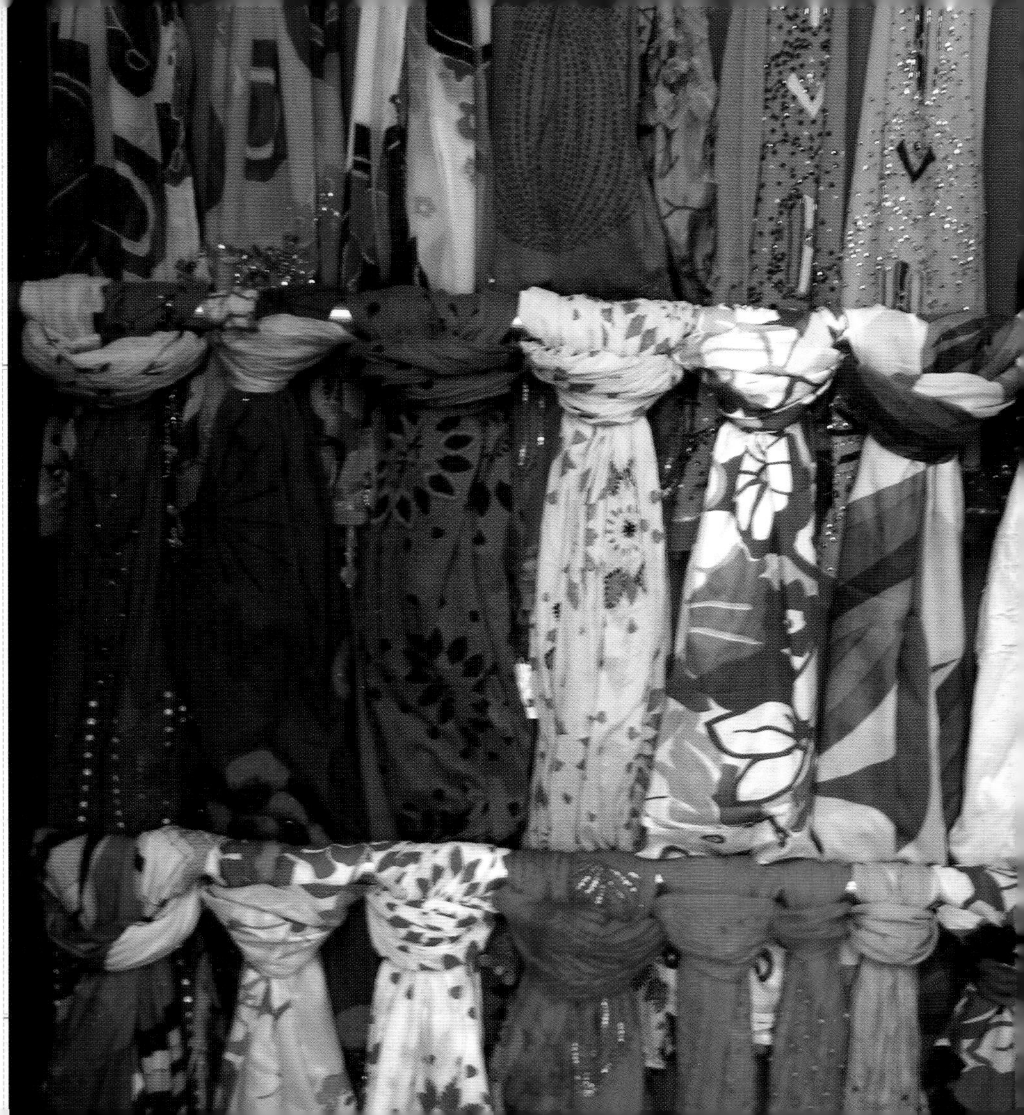

CHANTAL THOMASS

Women's lingerie holds as much sex appeal for those who wear it as it does for those who are seduced by it, something that Paris' queen of frothy lingerie, Chantal Thomass, knows well after thirty years of dressing and undressing Parisian women in corsets, nightgowns, bras, and lace stockings. Her story is full of turmoil. Her first business, Ter et Bantine, opened in 1967. By adopting a style verging on androgynous—a far cry from the fashion of the time that made women into objects of seduction—the designer's explosively colored dresses, hats,

and shoes were pure hippy chic. The Chantal Thomass brand owes its big break to Brigitte Bardot after the star made a purchase on a beach in Saint-Tropez. The first shop opened on rue Dauphine, and Ter et Bantine's very colorful "against the grain" fashion became exclusively targeted to the teenage market. With the backing of the Japanese textile firm World, the Chantal Thomass brand flourished internationally. In 1975, she was the first clothes designer to send lingerie down the runway like prêt-à-porter and to make garments with Lycra®. Fifteen years later, she invented the first pair of lace tights. Her nickname, The High Priestess of Lingerie, has stuck with her ever since thanks to her "underwear as outerwear" style and curvaceous silhouettes projecting exaggerated femininity. From then on she carved her own distinctive place in the industry somewhere in between ready-made

clothing and haute couture. Internationally acclaimed early in her career, the designer's trade name was taken away from her in 1995, but she then bought it back in 1998 in order to continue designing under the brand name. Things may be plain sailing these days, but there is never a dull moment. On two floors, inside a spacious venue, co-decorated with Christian Ghion in a style dubbed *jolie madame*, erotic fantasies and the designer's finds rub shoulders: bars of soaps, fragrances and associated products, and also umbrellas, purses, itsy-bitsy handbags, and some exclusive one-off pieces (made only upon request). You'll leave the shop tantalized, dying to slip into your lingerie and regale your mirror…not to mention your lover's eyes.

COLETTE

213, rue SAINT-HONORÉ, 1ST ARR.
Telephone: 01 55 35 33 90 • Metro: TUILERIES
MONDAY to SATURDAY 11am–7pm • www.colette.fr

Where would Paris be without Colette, the concept store that, after opening in 1997, became a showcase for all the latest in trendy, high-end design, synonymous with all that glitters in the City of Light? The 700-square-meter mecca, spread over three floors and designed by Arnaud Montigny, includes a water bar and grocery-store-cum-restaurant downstairs where a fashion-savvy crowd of stylists, fashion editors, graphic designers, and musicians can be spotted "doing" lunch, all happily slurping fresh fruit juice and eating salads that are "graphic design on a plate" and very "now." The ground floor has a beauty counter featuring fragrance ranges and the latest make-up collections in vogue: Hip, Aesop, Körner Skincare. One

look at the jewelry from Chrome Hearts and Aurélie Bidermann, sitting pretty next to the latest limited-edition designs of watches and sunglasses from the hottest up-to-the-minute brands, and you'll be smitten. At the far corner of the shop lies a book and music section with imports, magazines, and art, fashion, and photography books. Every month, the mezzanine's art gallery is also decorated with the work of "flavor of the month" graphic designers, photographers, or illustrators. Upstairs is home to an unostentatious hotbed of new fashion trends: designer shoes, a com-

plete wardrobe for day and night to strut about in, jeans, sneakers, polo shirts, and T-shirts. Everything that is exclusive and desirable is here. Colette (who has put her heart and soul, not to mention her name, into the boutique) and her daughter Sarah, equal parts discreet and elegant, take care of everything from selecting garments to putting together the ever-changing window displays that invite us in to discover another world, both modern and versatile. The cultivated classic mother-daughter duo takes pride in exclusively picking out avant-garde items before anyone else and skillfully mixing them with new editions of forgotten labels. As arbiters of fashion, they know how to make the most of an object's value in its heyday and consequently are big fans of limited editions. With this in mind, Colette has come up with its own magazine, *Le Colette*, featuring product launches, events, activities, and temporary exhibition listings. Colette doesn't miss a trick—the label produces its own selective and elite music compilations and signature Eau de Colette and Air de Colette perfumes and candles. Welcome to Colette's way of life.

FIFI CHACHNIL

68, rue JEAN-JACQUES-ROUSSEAU, 1ST ARR.
Telephone: 01 42 21 19 93 • Metro: LES HALLES
MONDAY to SATURDAY 11am–7pm
SEE P. 175 FOR OTHER BOUTIQUES • www.fifichachnil.com

Delicious! From candy pink to lemon sherbet yellow, gingham checks, a dash of leopard print, a smattering of satin bows: so much sweetness and malice make for a soul-stirring concoction. The fantasies of designer Fifi Chachnil reach out to the imagination before seizing the senses. Uplifting bras, knickers that send shivers down your thighs, curve-enhancing babydoll nighties, and spaghetti-strap tops…Inside these sugar-coated sweet shops of temptation with their precious décor, all Midas-touched and draped with voile, a few lucky men's eyes sparkle as they are allowed to accompany their leading ladies as they play Bardot, Hollywood starlets, or 1950s pinups.

This is where Fifi Chachnil showcases a constantly rotating stock of precious handmade creations, beautifully baptized "Youpla," "Dolly," or "Rêve." Your experience at each boutique is a bit different: The shop on rue Saint-Honoré lends a little room to prêt-à-porter, the rue Cambon shop is devoted to lingerie. The boutique on rue Jean-Jacques-Rousseau is the grandest boudoir of them all (also home to Fifi's design studio) where the atmosphere is at its most piquant and confidential: A fine black lacy push-up bra gives you the eye, a turquoise-blue baby-doll beckons you to reach out and touch its fine straps, a pink satin waist-nipper piles on the charm. This boutique attracts girls—and boys—like bees to a honey pot!

GABRIELLE GEPPERT

31, Galerie de MONTPENSIER, JARDIN DU PALAIS-ROYAL, 1ST ARR.
Telephone: 01 42 61 53 52 • Metro: PALAIS-ROYAL-MUSÉE-DU-LOUVRE
MONDAY to SATURDAY 10am–7pm

Always enthusiastic about something or other, readily whipping out her treasures on demand, bursting into peals of laughter, picking up the telephone…Gabrielle Geppert—the most Parisian German woman there ever was—has made her shop into a beautiful, bright, and cheerful living room. Set beneath the arcades of the Palais-Royal garden, this vintage specialist is well aware that she is living a dream: "Life spoils me each day and Paris gives me everything," the shopkeeper willingly admits. Art history studies, travels around the world, and brushes with fashion's finest talent, including Yohji Yamamoto, marked the beginning of her destiny. But Gabrielle's real inspiration is her immense love for clothes in all shapes and forms—from 1950s elegance to 1980s glitter. Since opening her boutique in 2003, this clothes junkie has collected things and scoured the capital's markets and jumble sales and other antique fairs every Sunday searching for a look or for statement clothes rather than labels. You'll be bowled over by the results of her finds.

Her boudoir is bursting at the seams with skirts galore, racks of blouses (Carven, Yves Saint Laurent), dresses made out of *broderie anglaise*, as well as towering emerald-green stilettos, all styles of boots, thousands of bags and purses (in satin, patent leather or kidskin, straw or macramé), coats, eyeglasses, and jewelry—a profusion of marvels in impeccable condition just waiting for you to drop in and fall in love with them and give them a second lease on life.

MADAME ANDRÉ

34, rue du MONT-THABOR, 1ST ARR.
Telephone: 01 42 96 27 24 • Metro: CONCORDE
TUESDAY to SATURDAY NOON–7:30pm

Size isn't what matters here and this boutique, one of the smallest in Paris, harbors more marvelous finds per square meter than many a Swedish megastore. Behind the name, which sounds like an old biddy's, is a pretty thirty-something who's exquisitely fashion-savvy, sexy, and perfectly glamorous. (The shop was named after André, star of graffiti art and nightlife scenes, to whom we owe the existence of Le Baron and Paris Paris nightclubs, the cult haunts for all self-respecting night owls.) Olympia Le Tan, a fixture on the Parisian scene, daughter of the famous

illustrator Pierre Le Tan, ex-muse of Gilles Dufour, and handbag designer, crams her nine-square-meter shop full of the favorite playthings for cosmopolitan fashion-forward women. The space perfectly resembles a girl's bedroom with its Hello Kitty, Les Bijoux de Sophie, and Adeline Affre accessories, flashy pairs of shoes, skirts, and jackets, T-shirts from Bapy, Eley Kishimoto for Ellesse, Maharishi, and many little charms. Olympia takes originality to the max by customizing a bag or adding embroidery to a purse for that pure Parisian touch!

MARIA LUISA

2, rue CAMBON, 1ST ARR.
Telephone: 01 47 03 96 15 • Metro: CONCORDE
MONDAY to SATURDAY 10:30am–7pm
SEE P. 176 FOR OTHER BOUTIQUES

You can't help but push open the door of any of the four Maria Luisa boutiques with pent-up excitement. What will we be savoring this season? What young talent has caught the eye of this Venezuelan woman who has it all—flair, spot-on taste, and insatiable curiosity? When her first shop sign was put up in 1988 at 2, rue Cambon, the capital was at last granted its own style laboratory. The multi-brand stockist specializing in cutting-edge fashion design has become a required rite of passage for all fashion industry professionals, whether they work with a needle or a pen in their hands. People visit the store to keep up with trends and also to buy clothes or put together a beautiful wardrobe that is timeless and appropriate for all occasions. She doesn't hesitate to

team opposites: an Alexander McQueen jacket with Balenciaga trousers, a glunge dress (half glam, half grunge) by American designer Rick Owens, and Manolo Blahnik or Georgina Goodman shoes with a Givenchy bag. Fashion aficionados and sophisticated jetsetters, avant-gardists, or smart shoppers on the lookout for good investments come here in search of creations that are often exclusive. With success has come two new boutiques along with menswear and accessories lines to complement her clothing range. Initially located on rue Cambon, the men's boutique and a shoe shop now reign on rue du Mont-Thabor. Maria Luisa's energy has earned her a fourth boutique, which is mixed and focuses more on young designers but that is still dedicated to the belief that "A unique piece is all you need to set the tone."

MICHEL VIVIEN

15, rue MOLIÈRE, 1ST ARR.
Telephone: 01 42 96 38 20 • Metro: PALAIS-ROYAL-MUSÉE-DU-LOUVRE
MONDAY to SATURDAY 10am–7pm

Michel Vivien wasn't born yesterday. Before setting up his label in 1999, the Grenoble-born shoe designer, who landed in Paris at twenty, was something of a rolling stone. Ex-pupil of the artist Pierre Alechinsky at the École nationale supérieure des Beaux-Arts, it was by chance, after a request from an Italian friend who had his own footwear brand, that he began designing his first shoes. Michel Vivien quickly made a name for himself, debuting in 1986 at Carel and Michel Perry before moving on to later become an accredited stylist for Givenchy, Lanvin, and Yves Saint Laurent for more than ten years. The designer's creations bear all the trademarks of his prestigious professional experience. His tiny boutique exudes an air of jewel-box luxury and enhances the allure of the very feminine, confidently chic shoes on display there. His shoes respect the bodies of those who wear them; the well-designed heels support the lower back. These

virtuous principles have ensured the brand's distinctive aura and worldwide reputation, which he has made available to Alber Elbaz for Lanvin. In his Palais-Royal boudoir, there is no doubt that you are in for a taste of the pleasure that comes from playing Cinderella for a day, with or without your prince to offer you your dream shoes.

MICHEL
VIVIEN
CHAUSSEUR
A PARIS

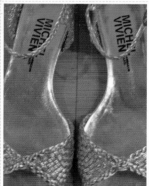

LE MONT SAINT-MICHEL

29, rue du JOUR, 1ST ARR.

Telephone: 01 53 40 80 44 • Metro: LES HALLES

MONDAY 12:30pm–7pm; TUESDAY to SATURDAY 10:30am–2pm, 3pm–7pm

It's a miracle! Corduroy carpenter's pants or blue cotton Chinese jackets used to be the wardrobe staples of all self-respecting intellectuals. But times change, and they've been replaced by a bourgeois-bohème set. By tracking this evolution in tastes, Le Mont Saint-Michel—an old clothing company specializing in utility wear—managed to make a comeback and stay true to its image. The challenge? Offer chic and simple men's and women's ranges in a bright little shop (sixty square meters). Using alpaca, cashmere voile, vintage merino wool, and Egyptian cotton, Le Mont

Saint-Michel came up with bright and cheerful hues to enliven figure-hugging cableknit sweaters, colorful ribbon-trimmed cardigans, twin sets, hats, and little moccasins and flats for the beach. A pretty repertoire of prints and plain fabrics at very reasonable prices delicately mixes the Parisian touch with hints of bourgeois provincial style. No style virtuoso will be able to do without them ever again.

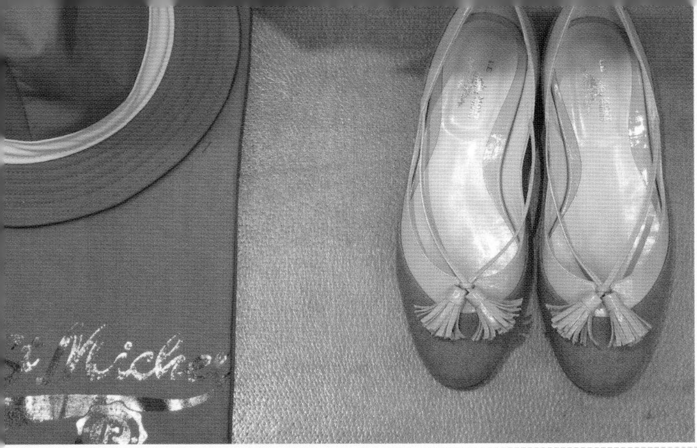

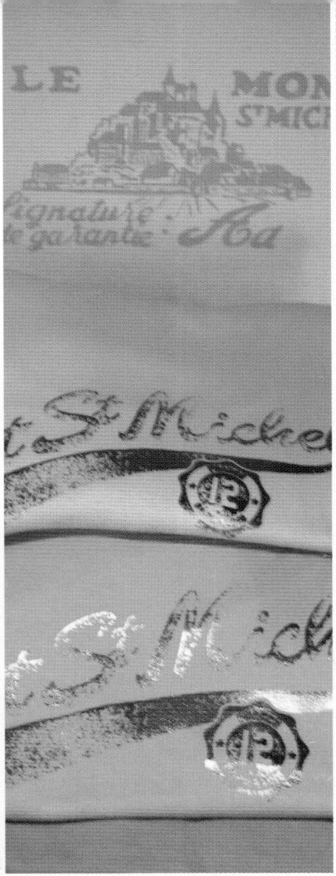

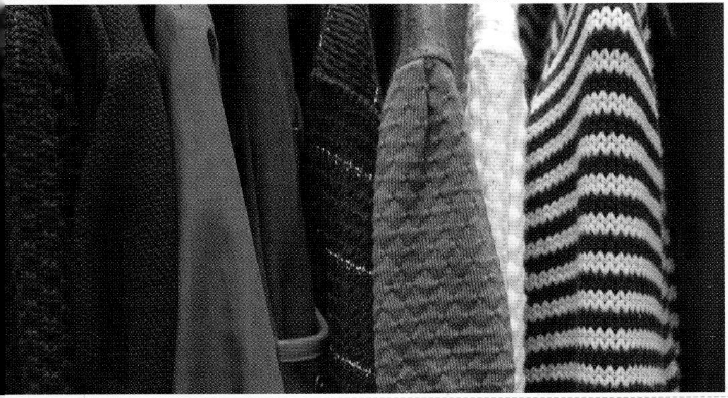

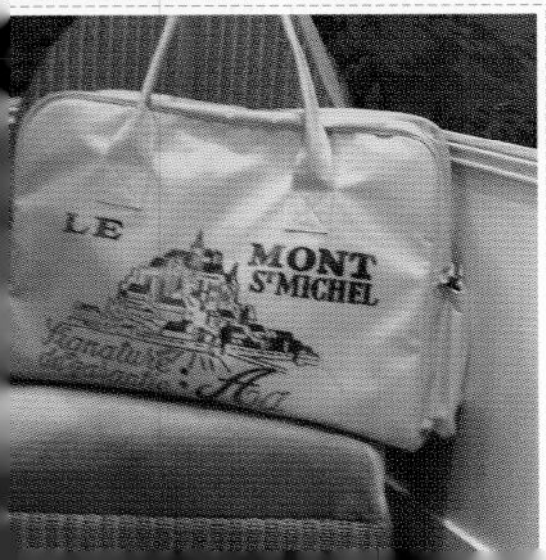
LE
MONT
S^T MICHEL

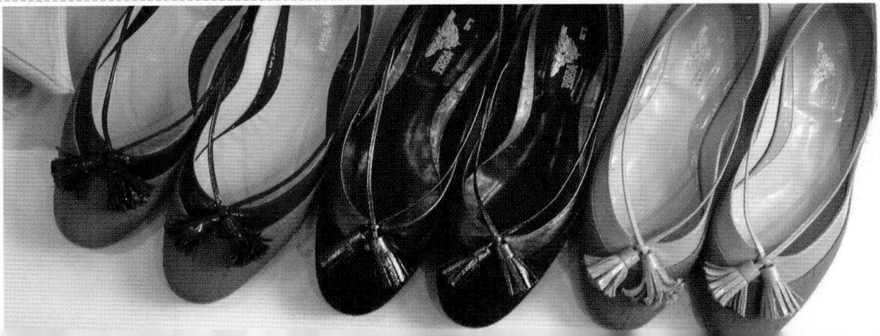

PIERRE HARDY

156, Galerie de VALOIS, JARDIN DU PALAIS-ROYAL, 1ST ARR.
Telephone: 01 42 60 59 75 • Metro: PALAIS-ROYAL-MUSÉE-DU-LOUVRE
MONDAY to SATURDAY 11am–7pm • www.pierrehardy.com

sleek monochromatic shoebox is the stage for this maestro whose work was until recently only available in a few rather exclusive high-end boutiques. Vertiginous clean-lined stilettos and also men's footwear, gracefully presented like sculptures to look their best, have earned the designer's elegant reputation. Qualified as a secondary school Fine Arts teacher, Pierre Hardy tried his hand at several trades (teaching at Paris' École supérieure des arts appliqués Duperré, illustrator for International *Men's Vogue*, creative director at the Hyères Fashion Festival) be-

fore finding his vocation in life. Backed by his professional experience, he went on to design shoes for couture houses Dior and Hermès. Each season brings a cache of finds that radiate radical femininity. Pierre Hardy is the only shoe designer (or almost) who knows how to gauge the perfect instep, the right classic luxury material (calf, patent leather, or kidskin), and the "in" color for each model, from a stiletto to a sandal. His designs, produced in small numbers, have won the hearts of clients such as Sarah Jessica Parker, Gwyneth Paltrow, and French actress Élodie Bouchez, not to mention die-hard accessory lovers. A must-see monument that's a stone's throw from the equally monumental Louvre museum. Fans can now get handbags to match their favorite shoes. What more can you ask for?

VÉRONIQUE LEROY

10, rue D'ALGER, 1ST ARR.
Telephone: 01 49 26 93 59 • Metro: TUILERIES
MONDAY to SATURDAY 11am–7pm • www.veroniqueleroy.com

Press "pause" when you get to a shop that sports a smoke-glassed shopfront and chocolate walls. With its many mirrors, wall-to-wall carpeting, and velvet, the décor looks straight out of a David Lynch or Dario Argento film. In her one and only boutique, Véronique Leroy invites her dedicated followers from all over the world to become more closely acquainted with her pure, clean-cut lines. This Liege-born Belgian designer knows exactly how to cross Nordic minimalism and Parisian chic with utmost elegance. She graduated from Studio Berçot in the late 1980s and went on to become assistant to Azzedine Alaïa, then Martine Sitbon. In 1990, she made her break by launching her first collection at Fashion Week. Bingo! Even with all the trophies Véronique Leroy has won at fashion festivals (government-sponsored Andam grant award in 1991 and 1994, and the Vénus de la mode award in 1994), she has never abandoned her purely inventive and creative style. Parisians who have had enough of girlie frills and flounces will find her collection pure, unadulterated, and terribly sensual. It features a wool cardigan, an androgynous blouse, high-waisted trousers, a silk crepe dress with cut-out detail, and fantastic new sexy swimsuits. Rebellious and fiercely independent, this Parisian dares to be different—and that's just the way we like her!

ALMOST FAMOUS

65, rue D'ARGOUT, 2ND ARR.
Telephone: 01 40 41 05 21 • Metro: SENTIER
MONDAY to SATURDAY 11:30am–7:30pm

Beneath this sensible-looking, multi-brand store where you'll find all the up-and-coming clothing and accessories stars such as Néologie, Bruuns Bazaar, Circus & Co, Louise Robert (purses and jewelry), and Elia Stone (strings of beads and earrings), you'll find the creations of new fashion talent David Hermelin. Professionals and initiated followers of fashion know that the design studio below the boutique (not open to the public) holds all his patterns, samples, fabrics, plans, and projects for his collections. In two years, the Chardon-Savard design studio graduate managed to introduce a series of labels before they were well known: Isabel Marant, See by

Chloé, Cacharel (that for a while had an address on place des Victoires). Keep an eye out for anything made with the designer's own hands in his attractive rue d'Argout boutique. A clue: This young man, who hasn't yet hit thirty, has developed a passion for stylishly modeling dresses into a second skin for his clients. His watchwords are jersey, silk, loose-styling, and femininity—finery that brings out the best in you.

EROTOKRITOS

58, rue D'ARGOUT, 2ND ARR.
Telephone: 01 42 21 44 60 • Metro: SENTIER
TUESDAY to FRIDAY NOON–7:30pm; SATURDAY 1pm–7:30pm
SEE P. 175 FOR OTHER BOUTIQUE • www.erotokritos.com

Exceptionally gifted when it comes to color, the Greek Cypriot designer and Studio Berçot graduate Erotokritos dares to be different with unimaginable associations that are irresistibly creative and elegant. Watch out all you coquettes out there! You'll be drawn to these boutiques like moths to a flame. You'll flutter your wings in approval amongst dresses that say, "I'm

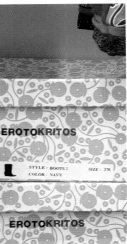

beautiful and proud of it," and lap up the nectar of a two-color top and a blatantly eccentric yet chic sexy pullover, or shoes that are as cutting edge as they are original. One thing's for sure: you'll leave the shop bedecked from head to toe; bad taste just went out the window. Strangely enough, Erotokritos seems to have a penchant for the Parisian palette. His new shop on rue Vieille-du-Temple—more stylish than the rue d'Argout boutique, and also more playful—reveals a taste for the

capital city's hues as seen in the pigeon-gray shopfront and the pavement-gray flooring. More than eighty square meters are dedicated to womenswear, while the fine Marais stone basement downstairs is devoted to menswear. Collections are presented on steel fittings and cement blocks, and walls are cleverly covered with sliding mirrors that transform into changing rooms. Erotokritos has succeeded in growing a flower bed of fashion on Parisian paving stones.

REPETTO

22, rue de la PAIX, 2ND ARR.
Telephone: 01 44 71 83 12 • Metro: OPÉRA
MONDAY to SATURDAY 10am–7pm

On Paris' most stylish street, barely a few *entrechats* away from the Opéra Garnier, you'll find a dance studio with a difference. It looks like something straight out of the Robert Altman film *Company*. Red velvet banquettes, immense wall mirror, hardwood floors, crystal chandeliers—all that's missing is the barre. Leotards, tights, and wrap-around tops are kept on long wooden shelves or on racks. But the stars of the boutique are the über-famous Repetto-label ballet shoes. This is a story worth telling. In 1947, Roland Petit asked his mother, Rose Repetto, to imagine a lightweight flexible dancing shoe. She gave him a foot glove stitched inside-out that Rudolf Nureyev, Maurice Béjart, and Carolyn Carlson adopted straight away. But it was Brigitte Bardot who, by wearing "ballerinas" in *And God Created Woman*, turned Repetto ballet flats into a garment that every girl would cherish at least once in her life. The Cendrillon (or Cinderella) model, launched in 1956 has evolved, now featuring the tiniest heels, plunging to toe-cleavage-skimming lines, experimenting with gingham, irridescent red, or gold. Serge Gainsbourg in-

jected a dose of masculinity into the brand with a shoe for the dandies of the time that would go with a pair of old jeans and a white shirt: "The Zizi" (after ballet dancer Zizi Jeanmaire) in soft leather, fine, lace-up, with a very slight heel—in white for the ultimate touch of elegance. As the years go by, the brand doesn't lose any of its power of seduction: French singers Mathieu Chedid, Benjamin Biolay, Bénabar, and actress Charlotte Gainsbourg are part of the fan club. Now—after Issey Miyake, Yohji Yamamoto, and Comme des Garçons—Catherine Malandrino has brought her vivid imagination to the brand. The boutique itself also dances to the *air du temps*, evolving its design and background music accordingly. Book your tickets for the latest show at Repetto entitled "Eternal Youth."

VENTILO

27 bis, rue du LOUVRE, 2ND ARR.
Telephone: 01 44 76 82 97 • Metro: LES HALLES or SENTIER
MONDAY to SATURDAY 10:30am–7pm
SEE P. 176 FOR OTHER BOUTIQUES • www.ventilo.fr

Since 1972, **Armand and Jacques Ventilo have followed their hunch** that a new ethnic fashion craze would pick up where the ubiquitous hippie chic left off. Armand Ventilo started by designing grandfather-style shirts, then came the long handkerchief skirts that he sold at Joseph in London. In 1986, the pair opened their flagship store on rue du Louvre where several floors were filled with their creations, with their pared-down lines and elaborate tailoring, as well as linen and ornaments for the home. They now run thirty-five stores worldwide, a commercial success that hasn't affected their appreciation for design. Their collections are always influenced by the Orient, Africa, and India in a successful mix somewhere between simple lines and poetic elegance without folklore. Refined prints, luxury fabrics, beaded, braided, and embroidered designs…Ventilo's difference is manifested in the brand's constant attention to detail and real sense of modernity. Pastel tones, vivid and subtle hues, exotic materials (straw, bamboo, copper) are recurrent themes in the store. The shop's aesthetic is Zen-like, and as with the clothing, features sophisticated finishing—a universe that salutes free-flowing fashion and reaches out to all four corners of the globe.

AB 33 AND NO 60

33, rue CHARLOT, 3RD ARR. • Telephone: 01 42 71 02 82
60, rue CHARLOT, 3RD ARR. • Telephone: 01 44 78 91 90
Metro: FILLES-DU-CALVAIRE
TUESDAY to SUNDAY 11am–8pm

There's no stopping the adventurous Agathe Buchotte, one of rue Charlot's muses who runs two shops, which perfectly complement each other. The first, at No. 33, offers the components of an ideal wardrobe, where many essential labels can be savored (Isabel Marant, Christina Ti, Hanii Y., Tocca) via a range of shoes, tops, dresses, jackets, jewelry, and delicate feminine lingerie. The lady of the house lovingly selects even the fragrances, adding that must-have final touch. The second address, christened "N° 60," is more rock-inspired and audacious. The beauty of this shop is that Agathe has a talent for discovering the season's hottest young talent before anyone else. Would this have anything to do with her fashion addict mother and her defined sense of style, with whom she used to scout for things for her boutique in Marseilles? Luckily for us, Paris is where Agathe finally laid her hat!

LES BELLES IMAGES

74, rue CHARLOT, 3rd ARR.
Telephone: 01 42 76 93 61 • Metro: RÉPUBLIQUE or FILLES-DU-CALVAIRE
TUESDAY to SATURDAY 11am–7:30pm

Going to Belles Images is like leafing through old issues of *Elle* with a style doyenne who points out the iconic fashion items worn by models captured in black and white. This woman would have to be Sandy Bontout, former buyer for the multi-brand store Onward and Galeries Lafayette. Young, thirty-something, and very stylish, Sandy is in her element in the fashion industry. She salvaged the shopfront and marble floor of a tailor's shop, adding a touch of 1950s to the furnishings. Be prepared for glamour...nothing but glamour! On the clothes racks you'll find a

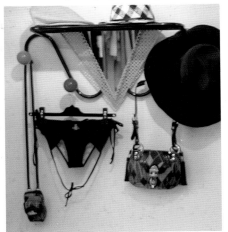

woolen gabardine suit by Vivienne Westwood (if you want to dress like a lady of leisure), a sun-ray pleated knit dress (very Bernadette Lafont in the film *Les Mistons*), or a little angora pullover from Le Mont Saint-Michel (so delicate, with a hint of retro, that you can just picture Claude Jade wearing it in a Truffaut film). High-heeled stilettos from Walk that Walk are among the range of shoes and on the shelves you'll find Bijoux de Sophie pendants. Belles Images is also celebrating the comeback of legendary 1970s London brand Biba, launched by Barbara Hulanicki and revamped with a vintage twist by Bella Freud. The boutique's changing room has the feel of a boudoir, perfect for an amorous rendezvous.

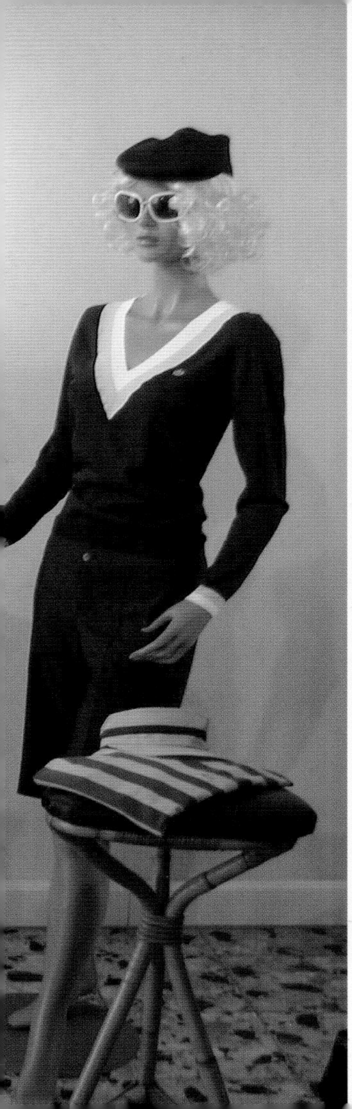

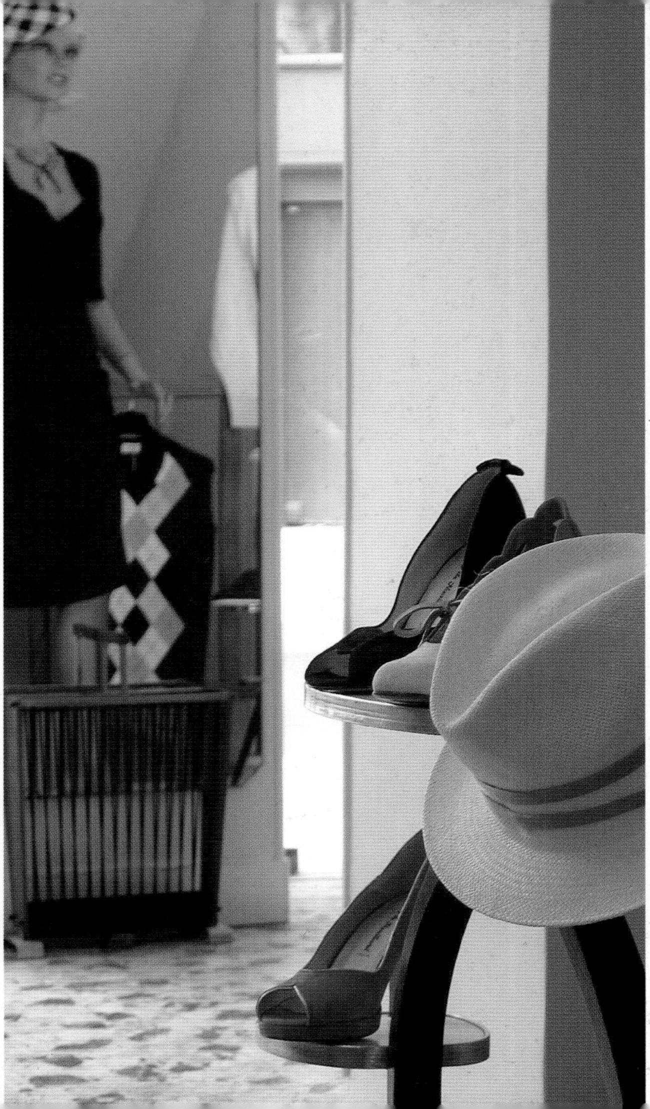

GASPARD YURKIEVICH

43, rue CHARLOT, 3RD ARR.
Telephone: **01 42 77 42 48** • Metro: **FILLES-DU-CALVAIRE**
TUESDAY to SATURDAY 11am–7pm
www.gaspardyurkievich.com

It was bound to happen! Gaspard Yurkievich set up shop at his home in an all black and gold "clubber's paradise" boutique in the heart of the Marais. This former Studio Berçot student, born in 1972, has fingers of gold and brilliant ideas. After working with the biggest names in fashion (Thierry Mugler, Jean Paul Gaultier, and Jean Colonna) and winning numerous awards, in 1998 Gaspard Yurkievich created his own label sporting his signature Y. In the meantime he was asked to be a guest designer of special small collections for mail order catalogs and the Monoprix chain of stores, which gave him great brand exposure. Gaspard Yurkievich's styling stands out for its conceptualized elegance, construction, and tailoring often inspired by contemporary art. Taking

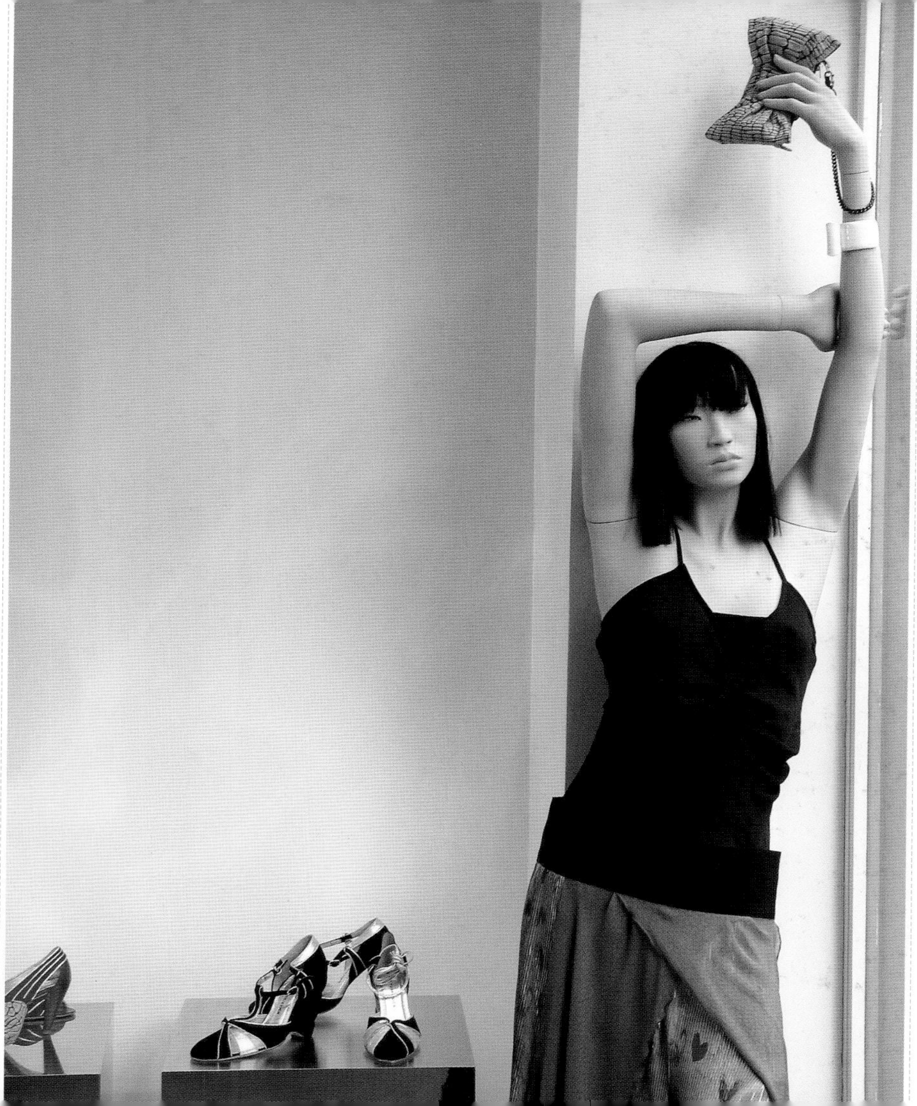

life in all its shapes and forms is the "Yurkievichst" philosophy. Audacity and a real lust for life and fashion are a must for stylish Y dressing. His baggy long-line, high-waisted trousers with wide creases brush up against little sleeveless flared dresses that fall at the mid-knee, always stylish. The couture designer excels in accessories (Plexiglas headbands with bows, stilettos or super-high four-and-a-half-inch-heel ankle boots verging on the extreme). Gaspard Yurkievich daringly plays with extravagance—and it works wonders.

HOSES

41, rue DE POITOU, 3RD ARR.

Telephone: 01 42 78 80 62 • *Metro:* FILLES-DU-CALVAIRE or SAINT-SÉBASTIEN-FROISSART

TUESDAY to SATURDAY 11:30am–7:30pm

~

ltra-trendy Valery Duboucheron's Labrador Twiggy knows very well that you don't come to Hoses just to pet her, but to check out the boutique's amazing collections of shoes, bags, and ornaments for the home. After years spent assisting the biggest fashion photographers as a stylist, in summer 2004 Valery made her big break. Once you've comfortably settled into her boutique with the aubergine façade, amongst pretty furniture she picked up along the way, there's nothing to distract you. You might find yourself seeking advice, or confiding in Valery who will guide you to the most flattering garment or shoe. Since anything that's chic in the world of stilettos or ballet flats couldn't possibly be missing (Avril Gau, Rupert Sanderson, Roberto Del Carlo, Gaspard Yurkievich, or even Marc by Marc Jacobs), the boutique is a meeting place for the most famous feet in cinema and Paris fashion. So here's your chance to experience some unusual, often impressive encounters. Jewelry by London designer Mawi and Natalia Brilli bags and accessories are essential finishing touches for any outfit. This is a precious, top-secret address.

MARTIN GRANT

10, rue CHARLOT, 3RD ARR. • **Stair A, 2ND FLOOR**
Telephone: 01 42 71 39 49 • **Metro: SAINT-SÉBASTIEN-FROISSART**
MONDAY to FRIDAY 10am–6pm
www.martingrantparis.com

he right time to call on Martin Grant is the hour before lunch. As you enter the building where his apartment-studio-boutique is located, your nose will be regaled with the smell of real home cooking. An appetizer, a promise of pleasure signed, sealed, and delivered from this razor-sharp master of scissors. Martin Grant left his native Australia for Europe well over ten years ago with nothing but a few ideas about fashion he learned from a seamstress, four years of studying sculpture, and a dashing smile. He gained a little experience in London while shadowing couture designer Koji Tatsuno, before venturing to conquer Paris. Now his little black dresses, well-cut trench coats, shirtdresses, three-quarter-length jackets, and revamped 1940s or 1950s hits have brought him a faithful fan club that followed him after he moved from rue des Rosiers. The turning point came in 1999 when Naomi

Campbell took his designs to the press and brought a flood of media attention, which would propel him to the status of a rising star on the fashion scene. Simple, pared-down, well-cut clothing made in France in bold shades (with very few prints), delicately figure-hugging while structuring the silhouette. Allure and nothing but allure! From one season to the next everything inspires him. His signature: an extraordinary interest in construction and his own unique way of designing directly on a 3D model. His role models—Martin Margiela, Dior, Balenciaga, and Azzedine Alaïa—all share this passion. Would coming from the other side of the world explain why Martin Grant has the essence of Parisian style down to such a fine art?

OLGA

45, rue DE TURENNE, 3RD ARR.
Telephone: 01 42 72 44 92 • Metro: SAINT-PAUL or CHEMIN-VERT
TUESDAY to SATURDAY 11:30am–7:30pm; SUNDAY and MONDAY 2:30pm–7:30pm

103, rue VIEILLE-DU-TEMPLE, 3RD ARR.
Telephone: 01 42 71 16 93 • Metro: FILLE-DU-CALVAIRE or SAINT-SÉBASTIEN-FROISSART
TUESDAY to SATURDAY 11:30am–2:30pm and 3pm–8pm;
SUNDAY and MONDAY 2:30pm–7:30pm

Olga is a guy. A surprise for some, but all Olivier Gampel did was take his name and make a girl's name out of it. His first shop on rue de Turenne with its jungle garden walls (metallic 1970s wallpaper) had the allure of Aladdin's cave. Prairies de Paris, Cacharel, and April May are the boutique's current treasures—but there is also old stock that Olivier has picked up everywhere and anywhere stashed at the end of a corridor: a dress made out of English lace that screams Chloé, boots, platform shoes, tunics, and chic strictly tailored jackets. In his second shop on rue Vieille-du-Temple, featuring David Hamilton lighting, sensual swirly-patterned carpet, and warm colors, everything has been designed to

accommodate romantic and glamorous women and make them melt at the sight of trendy Acne jeans, Marion Mille and Thomas Burberry's piquant and romantic fashion, bags, purses, and rock 'n' chic shopping bags by Xavier Denicourt. There's no doubt about it: Esmod graduate Olivier set himself the challenge of winning over the bodies and soul of Paris' most beautiful young women, under an alias. Mission accomplished!

RTA

3, rue CUNIN-GRIDAINE, 3RD ARR.
Telephone: 01 48 87 17 12 • Metro: ARTS-ET-MÉTIERS
MONDAY to FRIDAY 11am–7pm; SATURDAY 2pm–7pm
www.renetalmonlarmee.com

René Talmon L'Armée has come a long way. His industrial Gothic- and rock-inspired jewelry now adorns the wrists, fingers, and necks of many Parisian men and women. Brushed white gold and uncut diamond wedding rings; gossamer chokers beautifully embellished with a jade flower; long necklaces featuring several rows of skulls, Tahitian pearls, and silver feathers; oxidized chain bracelets with a precious vanity charm…René Talmon L'Armée handles jewel art in a way only a few people know. In his studio-boutique on the eponymous road that sits in the shadow of the Musée des Arts et Métiers, he has been inventing, designing, and making his creations since 2001; a venue decorated in antique tones where workbenches and a big motorbike sit in the shop window next to his precious collections. The designer offers a bespoke design service for special occasions. At thirty-three, before he focused on taking hold of his destiny, this young man had both experience and good manners under his belt thanks to his training with Hermès. Maybe in time this is where fresh young hopefuls will come to do their training.

SAMY CHALON

24, rue CHARLOT, 3RD ARR.
Telephone: **01 44 59 39 16** • Metro: **FILLES-DU-CALVAIRE**
TUESDAY to SATURDAY 11am–7pm

~

A small blue and white shop like you'd find at the seaside. Knitwear in all forms with a main thread composed of a playful spirit, chic, and a new take on the cardigan, the V-neck, sleeveless vests, dresses, and hot pants. After law studies at Sciences Po (school of Political Science), in 1963, Cairo-born Samy Chalon began working on his collections at Dorothée

Bis, where he discovered the inexhaustible resources of colored and twisted thread that he subjected to his aesthetic whims. Generous and sensual, Samy Chalon learned how to use knitwear as a sexy second skin, skillfully toying with forms to give his creations personality: dainty pockets, calculated fullness, never slipping into sentimentality even when he started designing basics. His charming, delicate sweaters are only made of luxury fabrics (cashmere and alpaca in winter and cotton in summer) and can be worn season after season without ever growing tired of them.

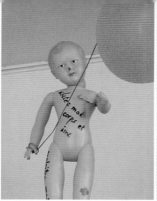

SHINE

15, rue de POITOU, 3RD ARR.

Telephone: 01 48 05 80 10 • Metro: FILLES-DU-CALVAIRE

MONDAY to SATURDAY 11am–7:30pm; SUNDAY 2pm–7pm

After five years on rue de Charonne where she was successful in her attempt to win over Left Bank fashionistas and models from all over the world, Vinci—the most Parisian of women, despite being Italian—became part of the trendy Marais set. Her chosen setting is an old pharmacy with a retro shopfront that she has transformed into a giant wardrobe. This clothes addict's deft touch has opened the minds and closets of her faithful followers to a new generation of talent gathered from all around the world. Providing a way for certain fashion designers to exist outside of the mainstream has become the mission this lady fulfills on a daily basis. Under the changing room's bluish lighting or in front of the little hall of mirrors reflecting your silhouette, this brand is about choosing between two wraparound dresses by Issa Couture or Thai label Stretsis, a top by Marc by Marc Jacobs or See by Chloé. How can you resist a jacket from English label Preen or a T-shirt from Fred Perry's Tailoring line? Tsubi, Rogan, Stitch's, and Cheap Monday…no

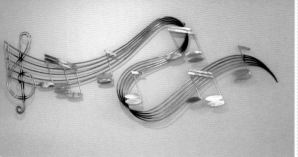

brand of jeans is missing on the list. Accessories will be the tiebreaker for shoppers who are still in doubt: Amaterasu, Givenchy, Michel Vivien, Marc by Marc Jacobs shoes, Repetto ballet flats, boots by Reagin, not to mention bags by Jérôme Dreyfuss or Minority …to choose is impossible! But if you're still hesitating, you can rely on Vinci's sales assistants for advice. Their points of view accompanied with such sincere *gentilezza* are sure to bring out your heart's desires, let alone the woman in you…

STUDIO W

6, rue du PONT-AUX-CHOUX, 3rd ARR.

Telephone: 01 44 78 05 02 or 06 10 66 14 66 • Metro: SAINT-SÉBASTIEN-FROISSART
TUESDAY to SATURDAY 2pm–7:30pm

The quiet rue du Pont-aux-Choux has livened up since well-known fine vintage specialist William Moricet arrived in winter 2005. Cloaked in a chocolate shopfront and a gold curtain, his high-quality apparel that spans the 1930s to the 1980s has been put together as a result of the acquaintances he has made, personal favorites, and the *air de temps*. Like in a museum, via some very fine and rare pieces, William succeeds in telling the history of fashion and different eras. This boutique gives you free rein to dream all night long about an incredible pair of Studio 54-style Azzaro sequined wedges or eccentric Londoners' elegant nights on the town inspired by a tartan and red leatherette Burberry sports bag. Studio W offers footwear that is always impeccable and nearly new, fun belts, extraordinary jewelry, and hats for special occasions. The accessories are a must-have. A place that will stylishly tickle any fashion lover's fancy for bagging a find.

TSUMORI CHISATO

20, rue BARBETTE, 3RD ARR.

Telephone: 01 42 78 18 88 • Metro: SAINT-PAUL

MONDAY to SATURDAY 11am–7pm

A star back home in Japan, Tsumori Chisato chose a modest street in the rue Vieille-du-Temple vicinity for her Parisian boutique which opened in 1999. The immaculate and über-simple shop is gallery-like (partly due to the stylist's featuring artists' work on a regular basis); once inside and past the corridors you find yourself in the kingdom of elegance. Everything is beautiful and surprising. In everything she does, Chisato affirms her brilliant fashion intelligence: impeccable lines, which negotiate the body's curves and angles to perfection, sound tailoring, a true feel for detail, pattern, and color combinations that are often daring yet always a success. Chisato studied fashion at Tokyo's famous Bunka school before joining design house Miyake

in 1977, where she directed the Issey Sports collection, shortly after renamed "IS Chisato Tsumori Design." In 1990 she launched her own line and put on a fashion show for the first time in Tokyo. Nine years later, Paris was the place she chose to realize her highly styled and ultra-poetic vision of clothing that today includes pieces such as a wool poncho with cloud and raindrop print, an igloo jacket, and a frothy rainbow-colored dress. This is fashion design with a capital F. Chisato also knows how to cater to modest budgets while reinterpreting a butterfly swimsuit for Etam or designing for La Redoute's mail order catalog. Among her fans are the very stylish Maggie Cheung and a few male clients who haven't been forgotten.

FACTEUR CÉLESTE

38, rue QUINCAMPOIX, 4TH ARR.
Telephone: 01 42 77 12 46 • Metro: RAMBUTEAU or LES HALLES
MONDAY to SATURDAY NOON-7pm
www.facteurceleste.com

acteur Céleste is a little piece of paradise at the heart of rue Quincampoix. Whilst on their celestial rounds, archangels paid a visit to the atelier-boutique and left a trail of unusual objects and fair trade products in their wake—little treasures for everyday use all the way from Mexico or Cambodia. Delphine Kohler clearly knew how to create an environment that would reflect her image—delicate, simple, curious, attentive, and aesthetically very sound. The designer became famous for her original take on Japanese- inspired flip-flops named "zoris" or "pattes" in heavy-duty leather with all-terrain soles, without left or right feet, which by a strange twist of fate are now a big hit in Japan. Nowadays Delphine Kohler prefers to devote her time and energy to passing on her handiwork skills to customers in her boutique where they can shop ethically and get busy knitting, sewing, or stitching. As the old Chinese proverb teaches, "Give a man a fish and you feed him for a day. Teach a man to fish and you feed him for a lifetime."

JOY

38, rue du ROI-DE-SICILE, 4TH ARR.
Telephone: 01 42 78 94 88 • Metro: SAINT-PAUL or HÔTEL-DE-VILLE
TUESDAY to SATURDAY 11:30am–8pm; SUNDAY 1pm–7pm

⌒

farrah Fawcett (who played Jill Monroe in "Charlie's Angels") and Aziz the Afghan greyhound watch over Valentina and her boutique with solicitude. Everything in her cheerful boutique, with original Marais stone and hardwood floors, was chosen with the belle's own faultless judgment. At the back of the shop, the dressing room looks like a cozy living room with its retro wallpaper and pretty dressing table that make you feel beautiful before you even begin trying on the clothes. Valentina's audacious and innovative choices are always in keeping with femininity and

comfort: purses and necklaces by Louise Robert, Alice Hubert, Anne Cécile, and Corpus Christi, Karine Arabian stilettos, Martine Sitbon bags. On the racks you'll find Stella McCartney for Adidas, Robert Normand, Fred Perry, Sonia by Sonia Rykiel, and also fashion by Maria Fors, Sylvia Rielle, and Evisu jeans. You feel at home here and there's nothing stopping you from bringing a couple of friends to share your finds and help validate your choices. Valentina also has more personal projects up her sleeve. This ex-pupil of the Esmod school of design has always had a passion for making jewelry, and sold her one-off pieces under the Iris and Joy labels before launching her own clothing range. Lovingly supported by Frédéric Verdier (designer for Néologie), with this her first boutique Valentina has got every chance of succeeding. *Bonne chance!*

MAUD PERL

106, rue VIEILLE-DU-TEMPLE, 4TH ARR.
Telephone: 01 42 71 30 87 • Metro: SAINT-SÉBASTIEN-FROISSART
TUESDAY to SATURDAY 11am–7pm
SEE P. 176 FOR OTHER BOUTIQUE

SEE P. 176 FOR OTHER BOUTIQUE

Maud Perl is so crazy about pigments that she captured 2,500 of them in her boutique in the heart of the Marais. Rare and ravishing colors for clothing with very simple lines: spaghetti strap tops and vests, pleated skirts, dresses, and baggy trousers for women, men, and children. For cooler weather Maud developed a padded effect based on an age-old technique seen throughout history on the cavalrymen of the Steppes, Japanese warriors, Chinese peasants, and the Rajput princes. All Maud's creations are made of the finest silks from Lyon, Italy, and England. Her philosophy is that "Pure silk or silk mix enable me to bring together today's

savoir-faire with tradition, different eras, and near and faraway lands." It's not surprising that Maud swears by globetrotting—she has learned Sanskrit, made trips to Bénarès, Fèz, and Istanbul. She has kept in mind the radiance of the world's most beautiful fabrics from her time spent traveling, and as she loves to share her findings she offers her customers a made-to-measure service, undoubtedly the only service of its kind in Paris. Maud is a woman with a coat of many colors, and her saturated indigo boutique will remind you of the blue sarouel pantaloons worn by men in the desert. As she says: "Colors are the fairy dust of adventure."

TRÉSOR BY BRIGITTE MASON

6, rue du TRÉSOR, 4TH ARR.
Telephone: 01 42 72 54 92 • Metro: SAINT-PAUL
TUESDAY to SUNDAY 11:30am–7:30pm

A volcano of color is currently erupting at this treasure trove of a store worthy of a Kandinsky palette. At Trésor, color is everywhere, from the shop window to the citrus bright orange floor to the changing room's fuchsia velvet curtains. In this multi-brand store, clothes are arranged by color instead of label. Brigitte is actually a magician when it comes to putting

things together. Choosing not to cater to one look, she encourages customers to create their own style and silhouette with clothes that she has carefully selected and picked out from complete collections. The idea is always to avoid a pre-fab look. On the agenda you'll find a large choice of brands from northern countries known for design (Belgium, Sweden, Denmark): Essentiel, Day, Rützou, Malen Birger, Just in Case. How can you resist such well-thought-out offerings? With a print skirt and a fine super-stretchy T-shirt, Brigitte can imaginatively do "romantic" by adding a quilted jacket, or, if you prefer a city-slicker look, a bottle-green option in boiled wool. Each composition is well-balanced; a real godsend for indecisive (those who can't buy four things in the same day) and inventive shoppers.

A.P.C.

4, rue de FLEURUS, 6TH ARR.
Telephone: 01 45 48 72 42 • Metro: RENNES or SAINT-PLACIDE
MONDAY to SATURDAY 11am–7:30pm
SEE P. 174 FOR OTHER BOUTIQUES • www.apc.fr

A.P.C. is the ABC of everything you'll ever need. In this production and design studio, Jean Touitou, born in 1951 in Tunis, and a Trotskyite fan of dandy rocker Brian Ferry, decided twenty years ago to keep his fashion simple, minimalist, and high quality. A revolution in its time, his first catalog was branded "neosoviet" and for his troubles he was bombarded with letters of insult. But he stuck with his ideas, and those he began with still infuse his concept of a boutique without frills. The same simplicity can be found in both the Right and Left Bank bou-

tiques: metal racks, direct lighting, plain counters. Here a jacket is a jacket and a pair of trousers a pair of trousers. It's all about longevity, being distinctive without being eccentric, finding your own look, never dressed up. Less is more, and such economy is the fruit of a perfect assimilation of fashion codes. Jean Touitou learned from his mentors: Kenzo helped developed his eye, Agnès B. his sense of purity, and Irié his feel for fabric. This singular and beautifully discreet man has been blessed with an inventive flair for dabbling. He was one of the first to edit a product catalog (which are now collector's items), to sell online, and to produce his own records and to edit his own accessories. An expert hand at solid couture and perfect finishing, Jean Touitou gives works to French design studios all over France. Couture "made in France" still looks set for a bright future and A.P.C. is here to prove it.

DICE KAYEK

10, rue du CHERCHE-MIDI, 6TH ARR.

Telephone: 01 42 22 51 05 • Metro: SAINT-SULPICE

TUESDAY to SATURDAY 10am–7pm

Turks at heart, elegant Parisian women in their style, the Ege sisters (Ece & Ayse), alias Dice Kayek, have been offering refined and modern fashion that is crossed with subtle—but never outlandish—Ottoman influences for almost fifteen years. The inseparable duo of jewelers' daughters, born in Bursa (the ancient capital city of the Turkish empire), have understood the *air du temps* and worked extremely hard. With the success of their two labels (Dice Kayek, the main range, and their second range, Dice Kayek Pink Label), they opened their first shop in Paris in an old seventy-square-meter former antiques shop that was given a makeover by *in vogue* Turkish architect Melkan Tabanlioglu (designer of Istanbul's Modern Art Museum), a venue awash with antique shades, and set off with a beautiful flower-filled courtyard. The Dice Kayek silhouette could be defined as a modern temple dancer: Full skirts are teamed with little skinny

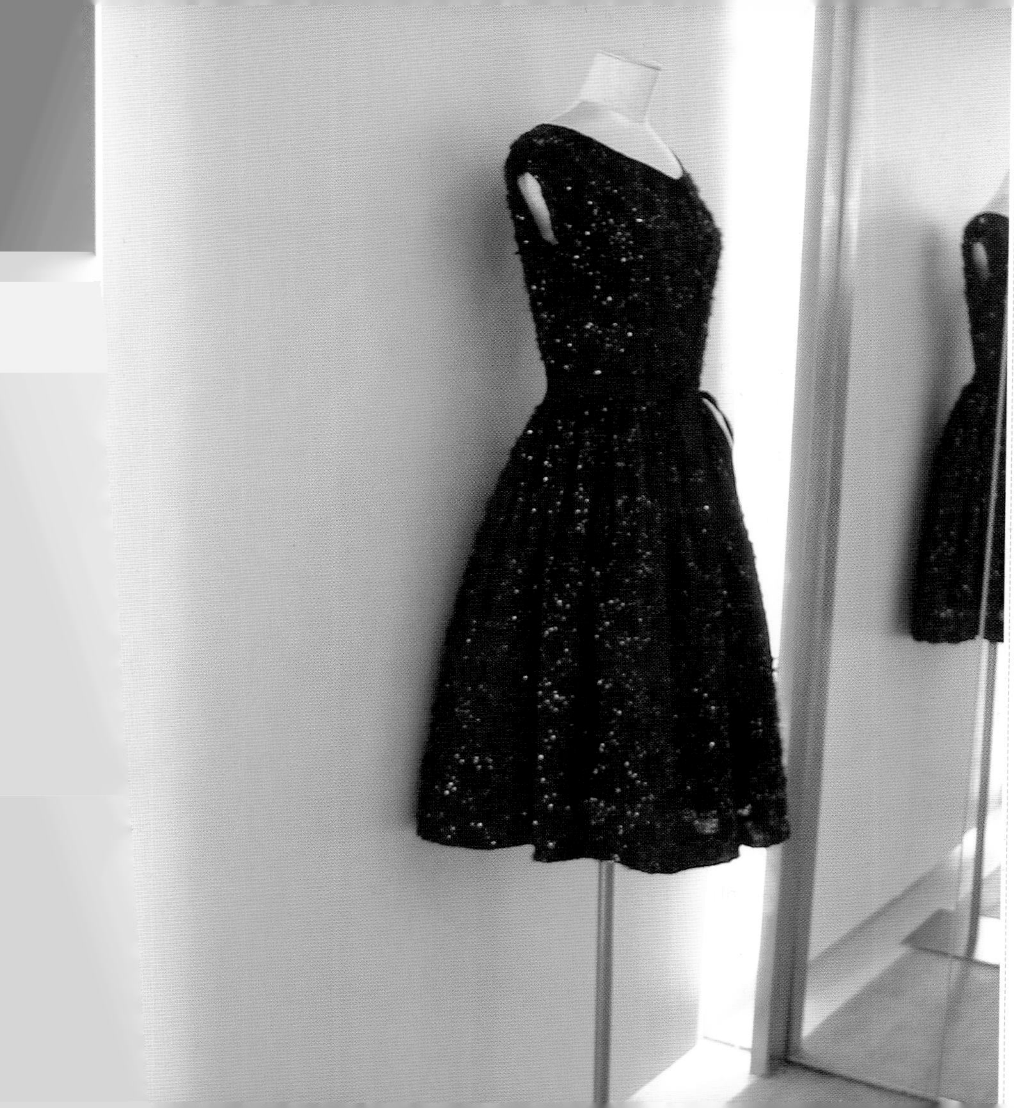

jackets, baggy trousers altered at the waist, and figure-hugging suits. Sophisticated dresses with poise are the label's strong point. Beautiful fabrics (tulle, taffeta, organza, silk) and pure lines always spiced up with exquisite details: stripes embroidered with bronze thread or a lace-trimmed cowl neckline. In each garment Dice Kayek offers all the refinement of the eternal Orient with contemporary airiness to boot.

KERSTIN ADOLPHSON

157, boulevard SAINT-GERMAIN, 6TH ARR.

157, boulevard SAINT-GERMAIN, 6TH ARR.
Telephone: **01 45 48 00 14** • *Metro:* **SAINT-GERMAIN-DES-PRÉS**
MONDAY to SATURDAY 10am–7:30pm

What if Parisian elegance was given a touch of Sweden? At this pocket-sized boutique, which has been next door to the Brasserie Lipp since 1973, we are almost expecting Father Christmas to walk out the door with his sack slung over his shoulder. This is where Parisian parents buy their children's boots, mittens, woolly hats, and rustic Fair Isle snowflake-patterned sweaters—and not just to wear skiing! *"Nordic, c'est chic"*: the elegance of a long striped nightshirt, clogs, boots (fur, flowered, or plain, matte, or shiny) no longer needs proving. As for Kerstin's natural leather summer sandals, we're still waiting for the next heat wave to be able to wear them! And how can we possibly manage without her famous stripy socks, gloves of all colors, sweaters, and bags? Kerstin came from Sweden in the 1970s, having dreamed of Saint-Germain-des-Prés, the height of Parisian chic. This queen of knitwear runs three other shops in her homeland; her husband Torbjorn watches over her extraordinary and charming Paris-based boutique.

VANESSA BRUNO

25, rue SAINT-SULPICE, 6TH ARR.
Telephone: 01 43 54 41 04 • Metro: ODÉON or MABILLON
MONDAY to SATURDAY 10:30am–7:30pm
SEE P. 176 FOR OTHER BOUTIQUES

Vanessa Bruno is a child of fashion, having been brought up surrounded by it (her mother was a model, her father had a hand in the creation of the Cacharel brand). Anything but what you might call a frivolous scatterbrain, she built her own label—which is now making waves stateside and in Japan—without fanfare, catwalk shows, or advertising, but with the steady determination to offer young women a look that's a little gauche yet dynamic, sexy, half-rock and

half-glamour. A breath of fresh air, warm if not a little hyper, this is one designer that doesn't go for "sweet," preferring strong instead. Her emblems include lisle T-shirts, mohair sweaters that in the designer's own words "give you an ample bosom," and a sequined canvas shopping bag, which became THE cult fashion accessory in one season and is still being snapped up from Tokyo to New York and in the Marais. With such high standards she only uses fine authentic "feel good" fabrics: silk seersucker, silk satin, or woolen jersey. Her tailoring features a fluid, feminine bust with defined hips. A firm favorite with magazines, actresses Vanessa Paradis and Charlotte Gainsbourg, and the high street (she has been designing for La Redoute's mail order catalog for about ten years), she offers a striking mix of delicacy, humanity, and no-nonsense styling.

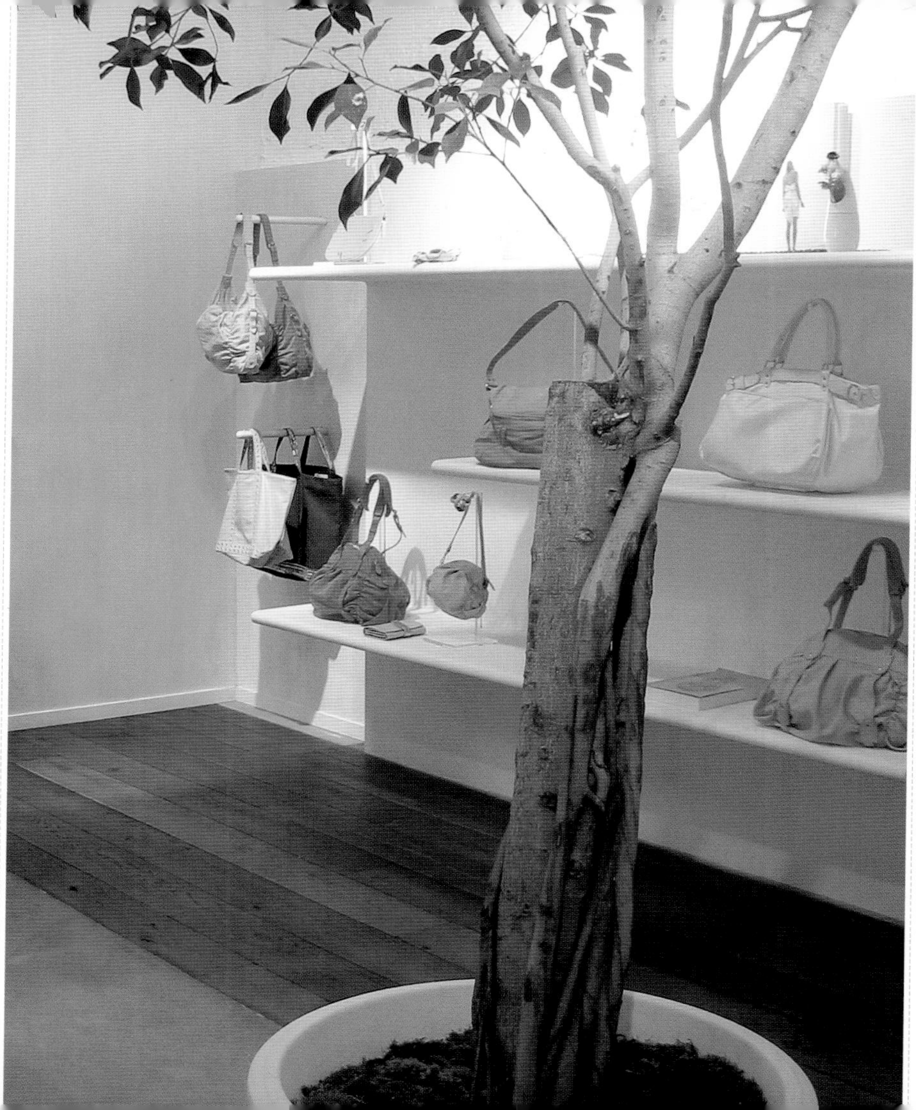

LES PRAIRIES DE PARIS

6, rue du PRÉ-AUX-CLERCS, 7TH ARR.
Telephone: 01 40 20 44 12 • Metro: RUE-DU-BAC or SAINT-GERMAIN-DES-PRÉS
MONDAY to SATURDAY 10:30am–7pm

I n the Marseilles of her adolescence, little Laetitia Ivanez used to watch her father make skirts out of gauze, plunge them in dye, then put them out to dry in the air like colored flags. From this man, a poet with many passions frustrated by the lack of greenery in his adopted city, "Les Prairies de Paris" was born. On the day of his first big fashion show, disaster struck, leaving Laetitia in charge. Determined to keep the flame of her father's memory alight, she kissed her acting career goodbye and struck out in his footsteps. As a result, the chatty brunette has been successfully inventing simple, cheerful clothes in colors from faraway lands (coral, emerald, Tuareg blue) for almost a decade now. While her famous two-tiered pleated skirts became wardrobe staples and have been around the world and back, some Parisians may remember the hype surrounding the ballet pumps she designed for André that were all the rage. Her well-cut clothes with simple lines—easy to wear at any time or any age, enlivened with details that ooze style—seduced pretty actresses Elsa Zylberstein and Kirsten Dunst before becoming a hit on the high street. Laetitia recently incorporated lace-trimmed stilettos and patent leather moccasins to complete her outfits, as well as a delicate and refined line of jewelry. Her fresh white boutique, sheltered on a quiet street, has sweet nursery-rhyme simplicity and proves that happiness can thrive on the prairie.

L'ÉCLAIREUR

8, rue BOISSY-D'ANGLAS, 8TH ARR.
Telephone: 01 53 43 03 70 • Metro: CONCORDE
MONDAY to SATURDAY 11am–7pm
SEE P. 175 FOR OTHER BOUTIQUES • www.leclaireur.com

L'Éclaireur is always way ahead of the game. At the beginning of the 1980s, Martine and Armand Hadida were the first to introduce us to casual style in their space in the basement of Marithé and François Girbaud's *galerie marchande des Champs-Élysées*. Today, with five boutiques in Paris, each sporting a steel and wood décor, they are still trading under their well-deserved name, which means "scout." Here you'll find the cream of cutting-edge fashion (including Ann Demeulemeester, Comme des Garçons, Martin Margiela, Marni, Chloé, Balenciaga). None of

the shops are the same. The one on rue Hérold is the most hidden of them all. You have to buzz through on the intercom to gain access to the grotto via a long dark corridor where you'll find antiques, shoes, and jewelry. An ultra-edgy look can be yours (Undercover, Anne Valérie Hash, If Six was Nine) on one condition: You're not watching what you're spending. The sprawling multi-tiered store on rue Boissy-d'Anglas that stands where the former Thierry Mugler shop once stood also brings together the finest fashion (Roland Mouret, Haute by Vincenzo de Cotiis, Basso and Brooke, Ken Scott, Alessandro de Benedetti, Guaglianone, Thomas Wylde, Marni, Dior Homme, Gianni Barbato), accessories, design, and home décor. You can even have a drink and a bite to eat. A fashionista's dream! The quality of the service and advice on hand in every language is remarkable all around.

LACOSTE

93-95, avenue des CHAMPS-ÉLYSÉES, 8TH ARR.

Telephone: 01 47 23 39 26 • Metro: GEORGE-V

MONDAY to THURSDAY 10am–7:30pm; FRIDAY and SATURDAY 10am–8pm

SEE P. 175 FOR OTHER BOUTIQUES • www.lacoste.fr

Ultra-trendy, the French croc is a star by international men and women's fashion press standards. Who'd have thought it? Lycra® fitted polo shirts, cigarette pants, and shirts are the latest hits of the old French fashion house that, since 2000, has been rejuvenated under the creative direction of Christophe Lemaire, Christian Lacroix's former right-hand man and sometimes DJ. His fashion philosophy: refined lines, high-tech and comfortable fabrics, solidly constructed collections that are original and always casual. According to the designer: "In design, the real revolu-

tion at the end of the twentieth century was rock and hip-hop music." The "Lemaire touch," consisting of vibrant colors (flourescent yellow, coral, absinthe), fitted tailoring, and affordable prices has given the legendary brand many happy days. The big round Lacoste boutiques revamped by the designer Christophe Pillet and the architect Patrick Rubin get straight to the point by accentuating what's essential—the clothes. For the famous 1212 model short-sleeved pique polo shirt (born in 1927 of the collaboration between tennis player René Lacoste and knitwear manufacturer: André Gillier, on sale in 1933), the future looks bright: Once a winner always a winner!

PAUL & JOE

2, avenue MONTAIGNE, 8TH ARR.

Telephone: 01 47 20 57 50 • Metro: ALMA-MARCEAU

MONDAY to SATURDAY 10am–7pm

SEE P. 176 FOR OTHER BOUTIQUES • www.paulandjoe.com

Paul & Joe's turning point was when Sophie Albou opened a boutique on avenue Montaigne. Behind the brand name Paul & Joe, the names of her two sons, Sophie made her career debut in fashion for men, to whom she offered a fresh colorful retro style that went against the grain. The clear success of her collections urged her to give in to the widespread demand for a womenswear range. In 1996, Sophie presented a small collection of shirts and trousers…and it worked. Season after season, the French Fashion Institute graduate puts her stamp on designs that are envied from New York to Tokyo. Little capes, beautiful vintage-style wedge-heel boots, tunics, bags, lingerie, and flowery dresses, this multicolored feminine wardrobe is on show in each one of her travel-inspired boutiques, with an ambiance that Sophie carefully creates. Each shop is unique and has its own charm, an experience

PAUL & JOE
PARIS

that feels like being in a family home filled with objects picked up along the way—a bookcase, sofas, 1970's floor lamps. The new Little Paul & Joe range (for children ages 4-12) now offers pint-sized editions of the adult range. And because fashion must hit the high street, Paul & Joe Sisters—another range about a third less expensive than the others—was born not so long ago. All you coquettish film buffs out there, did you know that "the world's most beautiful woman in 2006," the sublime Scarlett Johansson, wore Paul & Joe in Woody Allen's box office hit *Match Point?*

JUDITH LACROIX

3, rue HENRI-MONNIER, 9TH ARR.

Telephone: 01 48 78 22 37 • Metro: SAINT-GEORGES

TUESDAY to FRIDAY 11am–7:30pm; SATURDAY 10:30am–7:30pm

SEE P. 175 FOR OTHER BOUTIQUE • www.judithlacroix.com

Judith Lacroix is a level-headed young woman who knows what it takes to build an image little by little over time. After sound management studies and ten years of experience at Vanessa Bruno, Loft, and Galeries Lafayette, she set off on a long excursion Down Under in New Zealand. She came back with a desire that began when she was pregnant with her daughter: to dress little ones.

Bergdorf Goodman, Barneys, and Bloomingdale's in New York, Isetan in Tokyo, Colette and Bon Marché in Paris immediately placed orders for her designs. In 2004, she finally opened her first boutique, in the ninth arrondissement, a stone's throw from her home. The place has a stylish baroque décor: patterned wallpaper and an enormous Bohemian crystal chandelier, elegant and extravagant. The womenswear range which is classic (but not too classic) and trendy (but not excessively so), now

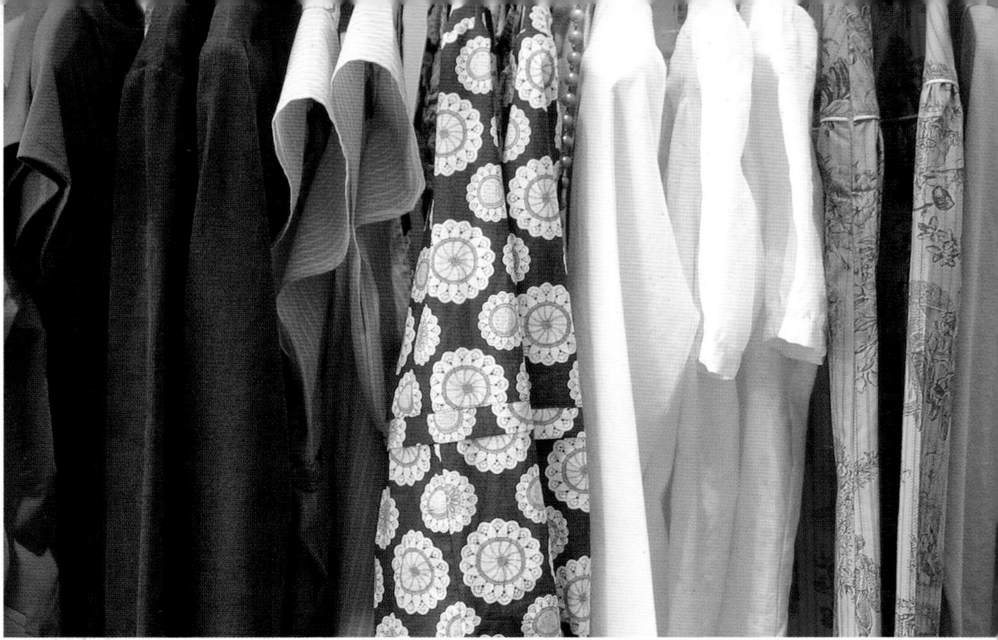

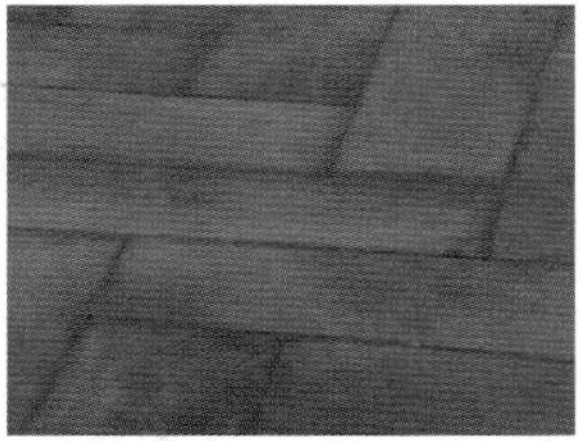

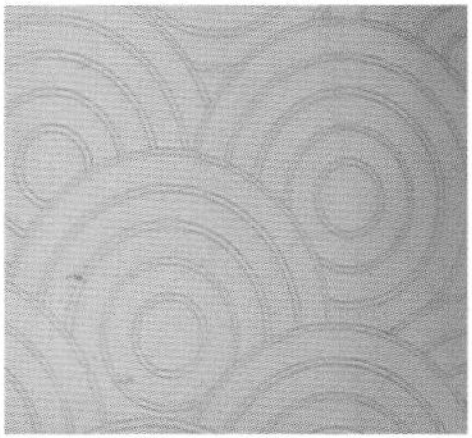

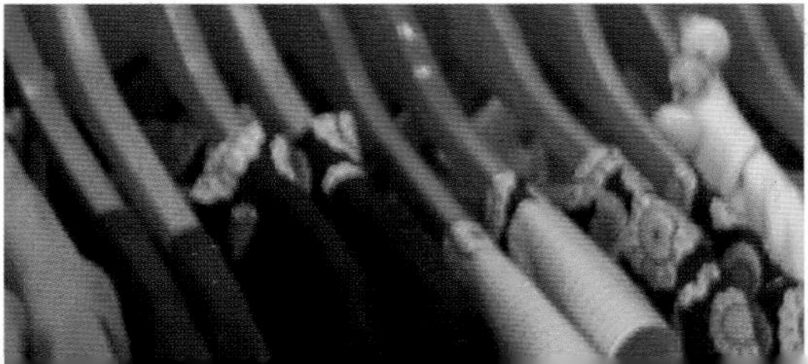

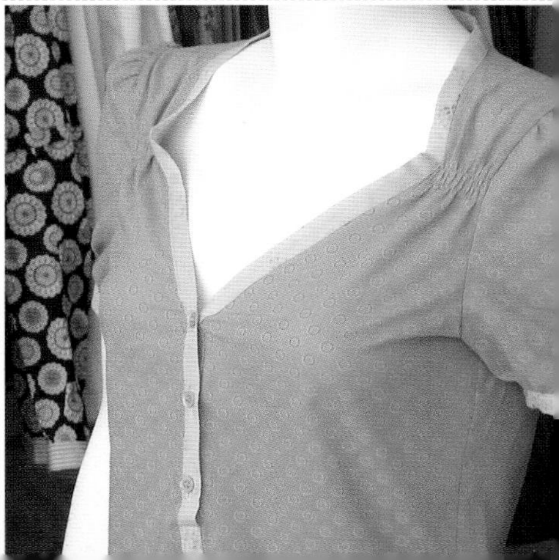

fills the racks. Judith's secret strength lies in the prints that she designs herself in limited editions, which translate souvenirs from her travels into soft shades inspired by her memories. She has applied her trademark graph paper motif (inspired by school notebooks that bring back memories of ink-stained fingers) to short-sleeved blouses, hats, and reversible dresses for little girls. Why do we love her so? For her tailoring, which conjures up dreamy timeless nostalgia. Homebody at heart, Judith has just added a small menswear collection to her winning children's and womenswear combo.

KARINE ARABIAN

4, rue PAPILLON, 9TH ARR.
Telephone: 01 45 23 23 24 • Metro: CADET or POISSONNIÈRE
MONDAY to SATURDAY 10am–7pm • www.karinearabian.com

A big shopfront and an elegant window display that shines in this rather industrial working-class neighborhood—a far cry from Paris' classic fashion circuits. Starting out as a showroom, it wasn't long before the Karine Arabian shop took on a "boudoir chic" allure, playing host each season to the young Studio Berçot-trained stylist's latest accessory line. Flesh-colored walls, scarlet ceiling, hardwood floor, tables, armchairs, and couches she's picked up en route, Karine Arabian knew exactly how to give the former locksmith's workshop the touch of warmth and sensuality that suits her style. It was during a visit to the flea market when she found herself in front of a jumble of pearls and pieces of metal that this tailor's daughter discovered her love for jewelry and her destiny was sealed. Working for Swarovski and then Chanel enabled her to perfect her savoir-faire. At thirty, Karine set up her own business and her own brand. While her

bags—a clever mix of leather and metal—stand out from the crowd, Parisians can't get enough of her leather and metal jewelry (still a hit!), round-toed shoes, purses, and bags, and since Winter 2005 her own prêt-a-porter range. Warm and generous, Karine Arabian bestows her creations with a fair share of strength and delicacy that you'll instantly fall for. Her accessories, which play with contrasting materials and a perfect grasp of asymmetry, have the power to enable anyone to put together a silhouette worthy of a diva, following the example of actress Isabelle Adjani (who happens to be a fan), or a busy Parisian woman in a hurry in soft leatherette stilettos fastened with an ankle strap detailed with a wooden ring. Energy and poetry for everyone!

MAMIE

73, rue de ROCHECHOUART, 9TH ARR.
Telephone: 01 42 82 09 98 • Metro: ANVERS
TUESDAY to FRIDAY 11am–1:30pm, 3pm–8pm; MONDAY and SATURDAY 3pm–8pm

~

When going to Mamie, a love for browsing, rifling through racks, and trying on clothes as well as having time on your hands are prerequisites. Here the clothes have history and speak volumes about their time of creation, and are a real living memory of the people who wore them. A multicolored silk top with smocking detail, a tail coat, an über-cocktail dress, a gypsy blouse, block-heeled court shoes, very authentic zip-up biker boots, platform shoes, dozens of bags made of crocodile or leather, and many one-off creations among thousands of other designer or label-less garments on a shop floor of more than sixty-five square meters. For fifteen years now, Brigitte—who isn't the slightest bit like a typical "Mamie" (granny)—grabs the most beautiful things she can get her hands on. It is not surprising that her clientele is made up of stylists, designers, and also clothes junkies who regularly call in hopes of finding THE pièce de résistance, which will inspire a future collection or fashion range or brighten up a dull wardrobe. In this XXL treasure trove, you won't believe your eyes, you'll feel giddy and maybe even lightheaded…but you'll be sure to walk out with a smile on your face secure in the knowledge that you definitely won't look like anyone else.

JAMIN PUECH

61, rue D'HAUTEVILLE, 10TH ARR.
Telephone: 01 40 22 08 32 • Metro: POISSONNIÈRE
MONDAY to FRIDAY 11am–7pm; SATURDAY NOON-7pm
SEE P. 175 FOR OTHER BOUTIQUES

Two hundred and fifty venues worldwide, boutiques in Japan, Lebanon, and Dubai, first prize at the 1991 Hyères fashion festival, prestigious collaborations with the finest Parisian couture houses (Chloé, Chanel, Balmain, Karl Lagerfeld), bags on display at the Museum of Decorative Arts in Paris…Benoît Jamin and Isabelle Puech have a trophy case to be proud of. The pair met in the late 1980s in between studies at Esmod and Studio Berçot, brought together by their desire to design. The duo have become icons of bag design. Their shopping bags, satchels, and drawstring reticules look like timeless relics handed down from an elegant grandmother, discovered in a street market in Zanzibar or Madras, or pinched from an eccentric old Englishwoman. Their former show-

room, rechristened "Inventaire," showcases those hard-to-find, sold-out designs along with the cream of their collections. The addresses in the sixth and third arrondissements showcase current collections, pure craftsmanship all made with extremely chic and sophisticated raw materials: ribbon, crochet, raffia, embroidery, patchwork, ceramic buttons, or pearls. You'll come out of the shop a little on edge, your curiosity aroused, feeling as though you've just come back from a trip all starry-eyed.

ANNE WILLI

13, rue KELLER, 11TH ARR.
Telephone: 01 48 06 74 06 • *Metro:* LEDRU-ROLLIN
MONDAY 2pm–8pm; TUESDAY to SATURDAY 11:30am–8pm

www.annewilli.com

As you're walking around the rue de Charonne area, near Pause Café (the headquarters of the Bastille set), you're likely to bump into Anne Willi. The bubbly Anne, born in Switzerland in 1970, is undoubtedly one of the eleventh district's brightest stars in fashion. In 1998, the Esmod graduate established her atelier-boutique on rue Keller before anyone else. Softness and comfort define the style; everything is designed to make you feel like you're at a friend's place to try on clothes, and swap a few ideas, or share your feelings about your last trip to India or your new life as a Mum. Her timeless zen-like feminine fashion suits all body shapes. Deceptively sensible dresses (low backs, splits, ties to do and undo), impeccable coats, and print T-shirts come in subdued and sophisticated colors. While Anne enjoys working with masculine fabrics, she appreciates color with prints that are like nothing you've ever seen. Rest assured her clothes allow you to be yourself, but you'll come away even more beautiful than before!

FRENCH TROTTERS

30, rue de CHARONNE, 11ᵀᴴ ARR.
Telephone: 01 47 00 84 35 • Metro: LEDRU-ROLLIN
MONDAY to SATURDAY 11am–7:30pm
www.frenchtrotters.fr

We've all heard a thing or two about French lovers; now we have French Trotters. Carole and Clarent leave the comfort of their own boutique to gallivant around the globe with their eyes peeled and backed with experience reaped from former careers in photojournalism. Each season, a town plays a starring role. After Tokyo and New York, Spring 2006 featured Paris. Eleven fashion designers, including Gaspard Yurkievich, Les Prairies de Paris, Maloles,

Burfitt, Indress, Néologie, Miséricordia, Émilie Casiez, Les Bijoux de Sophie, and even Petite Mademoiselle represented the City of Light with limited editions exclusive to French Trotters based on an Eiffel Tower theme. Clothes, cosmetics, shoes, bags, manga comics, CDs, and silkscreen-printed accessories selected during the stunning duo's travels far and wide, are thrown together bazaar-style. Upstairs, a multidisciplinary gallery reflects trends, and spotlights all kinds of artists including photographers, painters, and graffiti artists who tie in with the shop's current theme. An original way of embarking on great voyages without even leaving the pavements of the capital.

GAËLLE BARRÉ

17, rue KELLER, 11TH ARR.
Telephone: 01 43 14 63 02 • Metro: LEDRU-ROLLIN
MONDAY 2pm–8pm; TUESDAY to SATURDAY 11:30am–8pm
www.gaellebarre.com

At the Gaëlle Barré boutique, a certain harmony reigns that reflects the designer's style and life. This sensitive and sensual balance, apparent in the fresh and delicate dresses that have built the brand's image, comes from this young mother who can sometimes be spotted wandering the streets in the area with a stroller and shopping bags in tow. The boutique is a pretty girl's paradise. Winter brings tweed corsets, coats with designs woven in vivid colors, and hand-knit woolen tops. In the spring, fresh Liberty prints flourish, embroidered birds land on skirt hems, backs are bare, and waists slender. You'll feel an urge to start humming an old Charles Trenet song. Since 1998, Gaëlle has been fashioning rue Keller into a piece of poetry. She has also many friends in the area for whom she has made a wedding dress or a single garment. Ballet flats and T-strap shoes designed for Repetto that are fine examples of her own very personal style beautifully complete outfits in colors that stay true to her label. Her style—cool and refined—rekindles the simple emotions of childhood and the pleasure we experience as time goes by.

ISABEL MARANT

16, rue de CHARONNE, 11TH ARR.

Telephone: 01 49 29 71 55 • Metro: LEDRU-ROLLIN or BASTILLE

MONDAY to SATURDAY 10:30am–7:30pm

SEE P. 175 FOR OTHER BOUTIQUE

B ehind the star logo hides one of today's most exposed fashion designers: Isabel Marant, a tall dark-haired girl with the look of a Modigliani Madonna, who quietly made a name for herself ahead of her time. At fifteen she sewed up her first collection with Christophe Lemaire (who was fourteen at the time) and put it on sale in a shop at Les Halles. At eighteen she was accepted at Studio Berçot where she learned technique and style before entering the world of work with stylist Bridget Yorke of the ultra-trendy French brand in the 1980s, Yorke and Cole. She will

always remember the time when orders flooded in during the mid 1990s. All the young stars of the end of the era donned her long oversized wool or cotton cardigans, puff-sleeved pullovers, and colorful embroidered tunics. The secret behind Isabel's success? A disregard for snobbism, the pretentiousness that comes from a specific look, and the coldness that is brought on by certainty— and a propensity for—promoting the value of fabrics that are

mixed, modern, true, and full of warmth. Isabel's image, which often appears to be playful and offbeat (remember her yak-fur boots?), is a long way from the point-less sophistication of Barbie doll outfits. With age, the exceptional designer has gained wisdom and evolved towards a much purer style, yet she still pays close attention to current trends and women's desires. "I observe, pick up on things, and put feelers out anywhere and everywhere I go," says the designer. "I love to see where people are." With the likes of you and me in mind, the designer has created a more affordable line of clothing celes-tially baptized "Étoile," featuring many wardrobe staples. Isabel vows to provide clothes that are in sync with all occasions and moods that can be worn for a long long time…Merci, Isabel!

SESSÙN

30, rue de CHARONNE, 11TH ARR.
Telephone: 01 48 06 55 66 • Metro: LEDRU-ROLLIN
MONDAY 2pm–7:30pm; TUESDAY to SATURDAY 11am–7:30pm
www.sessun.com

Emma François, Sessùn's fashion designer, has three passions—Paris' Bastille district, Canebière (the boulevard in Marseilles), and Latin America—and is all the better for it. From her native Marseilles she has brought us refreshing feminine fashion with an urbanwear touch. Sessùn tailoring is practical, basic, and nicely fitted (trench coats, straight-leg trousers in denim or cotton fabrics, spaghetti-strap dresses with smocking detail at the bust, V-neck jumpers with slightly butterfly-winged sleeves, satin vest tops with tiny buttons that can be worn as outerwear). The brand's fetish fabrics are cotton, denim… and fabric used to make parachutes that Emma uses in powdery shades (faded pink, sandstone, white, sea-green, soft coral). You'll also find stripes, tiny flowers, and polka dots in each of her collections. As part of her master's degree in Anthropological Economics, at twenty-

two the outstanding student explored the South American continent. She discovered that each country has its own talent: Guatemala's was crochet, Ecuador's pure wool knit, and Peru's alpaca. Emma was smitten with the craftsmanship and raw materials. All this entailed successive trips back and forth. Each time her suitcases were full-to-bursting with designs that she had made over there. Success came quickly for Sessùn. Emma is now running her own prosperous small business and sends her work to be manufactured in Italy, Tunisia, and France, letting her designs be her guide while watching her twins grow up. Long live Sessùn.

143

LOUISON

20, rue SAINT-NICOLAS, 12TH ARR.
Telephone: 01 43 44 02 62 • Metro: LEDRU-ROLLIN
TUESDAY to SATURDAY 11:30am–7pm

J acques and Agnès, who are happiest when in the city or in their boutique, are a couple of modern leather goods dealers. Well, almost; they happen to make bags, totes, purses, satchels, shoes, as well as quirky little urban accessories for our four-legged friends. They give leather a new spin with denim fabric, felt, and many other inventive materials such as sparkly or

glittery cotton, which has become their best-selling fabric. Their little Post-it-colored shopping bags available at Colette stores have made a name for them in Paris and Tokyo alike. The success was carried on by their ultra-flat leather moccasins featuring two eye-like eyelets embellishing their pointed toe that made the wearer's feet look like little mice running along. While Jacques uses his eagle eye to pick up ideas, Agnès pilots the production. Their attractive shop on rue Saint-Nicolas is a real living space: workshop at the back, apartment above, and a courtyard that serves as a party venue where all the neighbors celebrate the coming of summer. Their chic impish accessories embody the couple's exceedingly Parisian touch—somewhere in between tradition and innovation—in coquettish wardrobes practically all around the world.

KOMPLEX

118, rue de LONGCHAMP, 16TH ARR.

Telephone: 01 44 05 38 33 • **Metro: RUE-DE-LA-POMPE**

TUESDAY to FRIDAY 10am–7pm; MONDAY and SATURDAY 10:30am–7pm

When the Renoma brothers (sons of a confectioner) opened their first boutique on rue de la Pompe in the mid 1960s, it was an instant success. The NAP (Neuilly-Auteuil-Passy) and Bon Chic Bon Genre sets, champagne socialists, and those who you might call bourgeois bohème, alias "bobos," were immediately taken and were crazy about Komplex's slim-fitting striped velvet jackets, which, as a guide noted at the time, gave them "Kennedy style." Stéphanie Renoma, École supérieure d'art moderne and Esmod school of design graduate, is hence the daughter of…but she doesn't let it get in the way of her taste and creativity in the slightest. The boutique that she opened two years ago with her husband, where she presents her label's creations, is living proof. For five years now, the duo have designed a collection called Ni-Search, a clothing line that they termed luxury sports-

wear. Jersey weave is their star fabric, whereas their detailing (studs, tattoo prints, Swarovski stones) characterizes their style. A second clothing line exclusively designed for the boutique, Ni-Search Paris, features silk jackets, dresses, and tunics. Finally, for winter there are blouson-jackets and chamois leather jackets, one-off pieces customized with studs, feathers, and ethnic jewelry. Alongside these collections you'll find a whirlwind of other labels. Seventeen brands of jeans, ranging in style from hard rock to hippie chic, from super-trendy Tsubi to Kate Moss-favorite Superfine and the latest hit from the USA, Paige Premium. There's also a slick selection of a few other labels: Dice Kayek, muslin Hidy n' J print dresses, and tops from Italian brands Trust Toilet or Paola Frani. Every two months, new collections take over from previous ones, and on top of that there's always something going on in this shop. What a family!

ZADIG & VOLTAIRE

16 bis, rue de PASSY, 16TH ARR.
Telephone: 01 45 25 04 07 • Metro: PASSY
MONDAY 1pm–7:30pm; TUESDAY to SATURDAY 10:30am–7pm
SEE P. 177 FOR OTHER BOUTIQUES • **www.zadig-et-voltaire.com**

With Zadig & Voltaire you're guaranteed a wardrobe that will never fail. Saying that the basics created by Amélie and Thierry Gillier's label (launched in 1997) are worn by the rich and famous, and pretty girls in the street, is a statement of the obvious! In less than ten years, the clever duo opened more than ten shops in the capital and has known exactly how to make a name for its very own brand of luxury casual style. Not to be missed: their legendary Atsui cashmere V-neck sweater or the Réglisse model which features three buttons on the side, timeless pieces that can now be made to measure in your favorite color or bearing an inscription that best matches your mood of the moment. T-shirts, perfect for everyday wear—blues, mauves, or the season's grays—are both comfortable and chic, and can be teamed with earrings and necklaces simply called "mypetitJewelsdeLuxe." Always *au courant*, the Gillier siblings have capitalized on the current lingerie craze in their playful modern underwear line, which can be worn as outerwear, day or night, with attitude. The brand's chic boutiques have been stripped of all affectation, leaving only the essential: fashion for its time in its prime. Come on, Voltaire, you've got something to smile about—your beloved Zadig is alive and kicking!

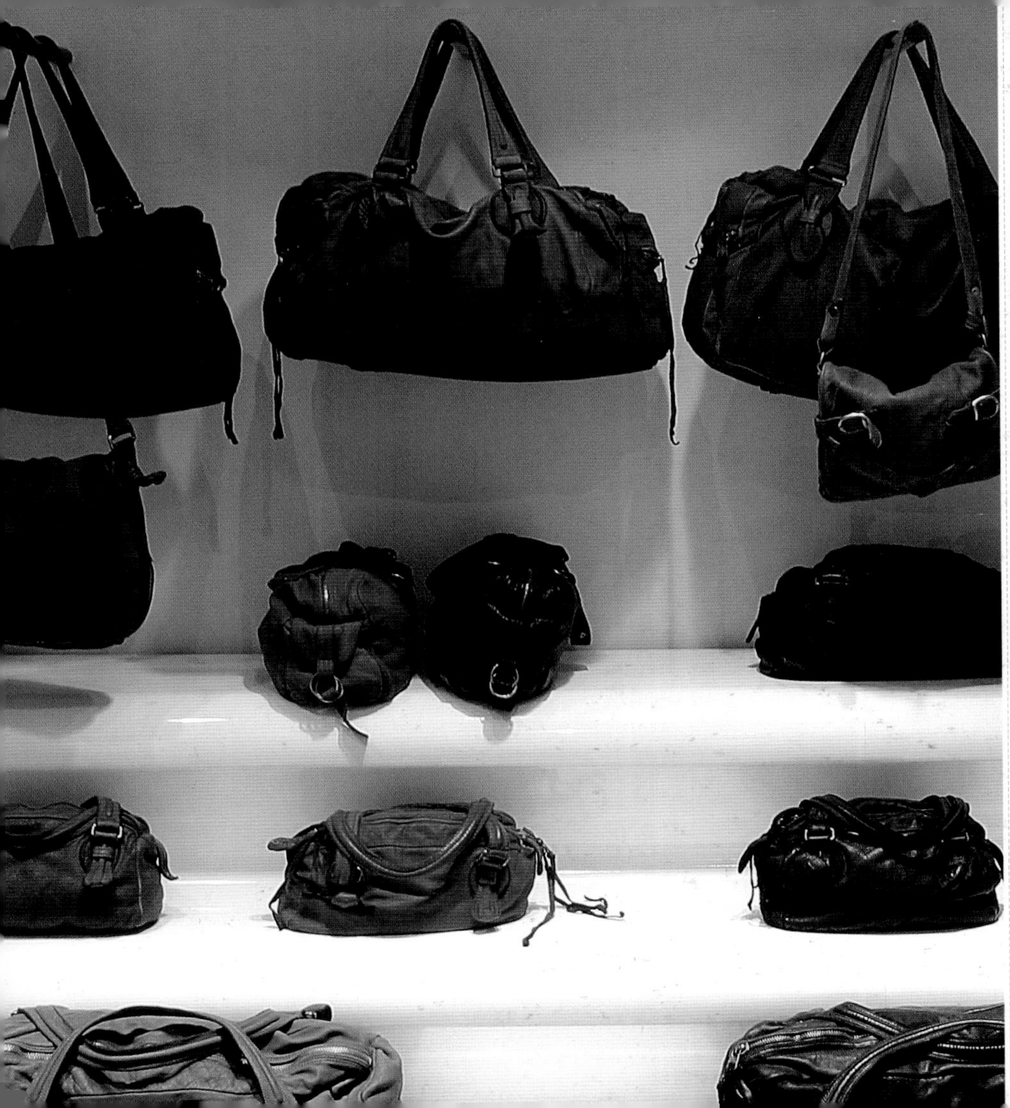

SÉRIE LIMITÉE

20, rue HOUDON, 18TH ARR.
Telephone: 01 42 55 40 85 • Metro: ABBESSES
TUESDAY to SATURDAY 11am–7:30pm; SUNDAY 3pm–7pm

O n a pretty little slanted street in Montmartre, in their shop with fuchsia and orange walls, Magali Legal-Schnubel and Valérie Martin proved they had what it takes to create a universe that is 100% feminine. Outside of the fashion mainstream, the two designers showcase original, often exclusive, pieces that are made for some of their customers on request

in limited editions. You've got to hand it to the two partners for their real talent and almost flawless instinct for spotting young talent. They have often been the first to launch and support the labels that our wardrobes know and love: Hannoh, Erotokritos, Marci N'oum, Circus, Aoyama Itchome, Néologie, Bérénice, and David Hermelin. Their selection of jewelry does not detract from the shop's style—how can you resist the elegant long necklaces and earrings by Louise Robert or Matières à Réflexion purses and other pretty bags, Japanese designer Rin's accessories, or Aconit Napel's retro glam? This is a multi-brand store that's just how we like them with all the charm and femininity that goes with a passion for the risqué.

SPREE

1, rue de SAINT-SIMON, 7TH ARR.
Telephone: 01 42 22 05 04 • Metro: RUE-DU-BAC or SOLFÉRINO
MONDAY to FRIDAY 10:30am–7pm; SATURDAY 11am–7:30pm

16, rue LA VIEUVILLE, 18TH ARR.
Telephone: 01 42 23 41 40 • Metro: ABBESSES
MONDAY 2pm–7pm; TUESDAY to SATURDAY 11am–7:30pm

Aptly named Spree—this is definitely the place for an extravagant shopping spree…The eccentric, the unexpected, and the refined best define the taste of Roberta Oprandi and her artist husband Bruno Hadjadj's finds. Their cosmopolitan eclecticism extends to the selection of clothes and accessories right through to the vintage furniture from the 1950-80s, photography books, records, and works of art they sell in their shop. In this slightly higgledy-piggledy, but never untidy boutique you'll come across an Isabel Marant top, or a dress by Christian Wijnants, a pair of Acne or Notify jeans, a Kristina Ti skirt, a Tsumori Chisato jumper, a Misaharada hat (a hit with Hollywood stars) with a 45 r.p.m. record by Peter Von Poehl, a Guy Bourdin catalog, a

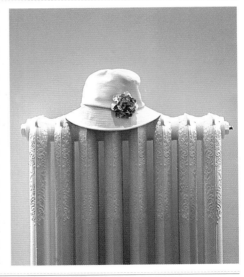

Hans Wagner armchair, or a table by Dutch designer Friso Kramer—all under one roof. Roberta, who is always ready to lend an ear, will gently and insightfully guide you around her collection, giving advice to suit your personality as a friend would. Labels resonate and trip off her tongue like the lyrics of an Italian song. The transalpine beauty has built up a network of client-friends that you may well bump into. From their first address on rue La Vieuville (a big gallery-cum-boutique) at the top of Abbesses, the couple moved to summer pastures on rue de Saint-Simon, near rue du Bac. Alas, due to lack of space, the new smaller and cozier store focuses on the clothes and accessories. *Rive gauche* or *Rive droite*, the Spree spirit is still alive.

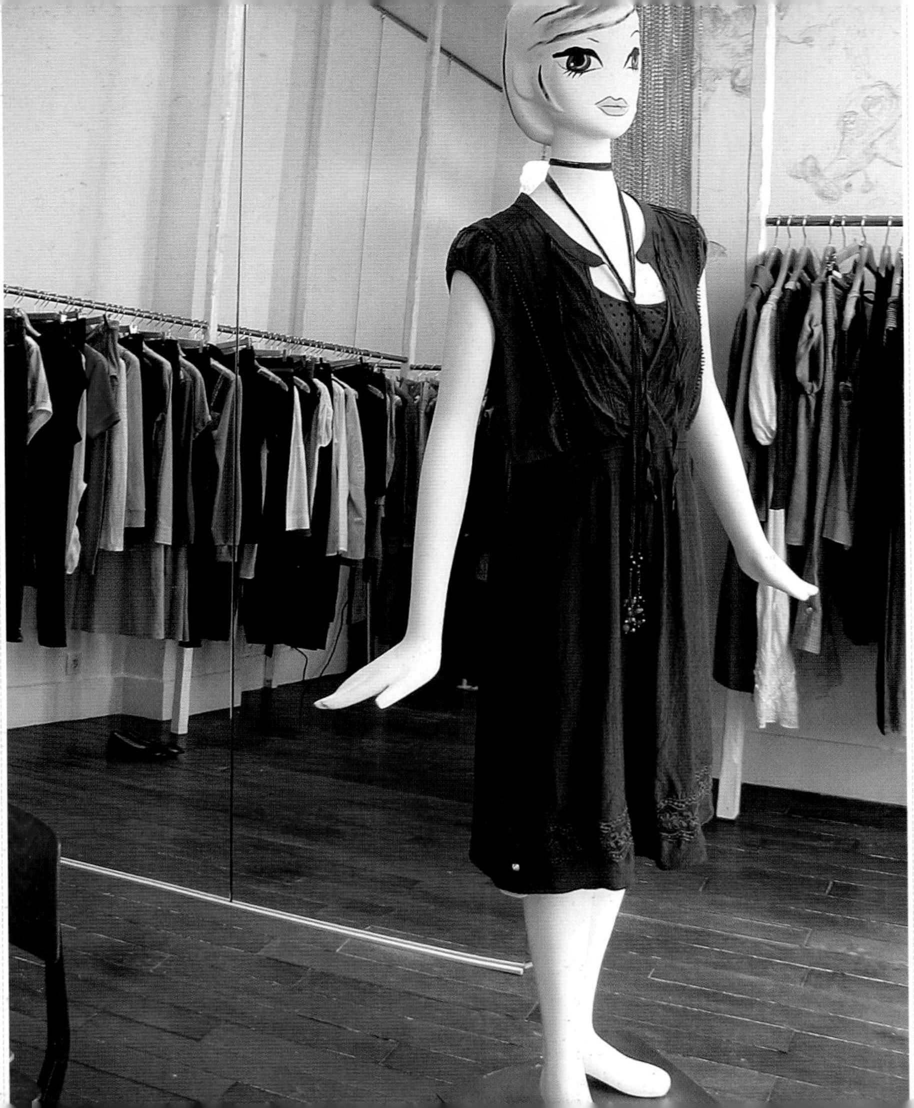

ADDITIONAL BOUTIQUES

Agnès B.

2, rue du Jour, 1st arr. (C)
T: 01 40 39 96 88 • RER: Les Halles

3, rue du Jour, 1st arr. (M)
T: 01 42 33 04 13 • RER: Les Halles

19, rue du Jour, 1st arr. (B)
T: 01 42 33 27 34 • RER: Les Halles

83, rue d'Assas, 6th arr. (C)
T: 01 43 54 69 21 • M: Port-Royal

13, rue Michelet, 6th arr. (W)
T: 01 46 33 70 20 • M: Port-Royal

6, rue du Vieux-Colombier, 6th arr. (M)
T: 01 44 39 02 60 • M: Saint-Sulpice

10-12, rue du Vieux-Colombier, 6th arr. (W)
T: 01 45 49 02 05 • M: Saint-Sulpice

1, rue Dieu, 10th arr. (sportswear)
T: 01 42 03 47 99 • M: République

Cour Saint-Emilion, wine storehouse No. 5,
12th arr. (mixed inventory)
T: 01 43 47 36 59 • M: Cour-Saint-Emilion

17, avenue pierre-1er-de-Serbie, 16th arr. (W)
T: 01 40 70 04 01 • M: Iéna

American Apparel

123, rue Vieille-du-Temple, 3rd arr.
T: 01 44 54 33 44 • M: Saint-Sébastien-Froissart

41, rue du Temple, 4th arr.
T: 01 42 74 71 03 • M: Hotel-de-Ville

7, rue Gozlin, 6th arr.
T: 01 40 46 02 00 • M: Saint-Germain-des-Prés

10, rue Beaurepaire, 10th arr.
T: 01 42 49 50 01 • M: République

Antik Batik

20, rue Mabillon, 6th arr.
T: 01 43 26 02 28 • M: Mabillon

A.P.C.

112, rue Vieille-du-Temple, 3rd arr. (W, M, C)
T: 01 42 78 18 02 • M: Saint-Sébastien-Froissart

3, rue de Fleurus, 6th arr. (W)
T: 01 42 22 12 77 • M: Rennes or Saint-Placide

Surplus: 45, rue Madame, 6th arr.
T: 01 45 48 43 71 • M: Rennes or Saint-Placide

L'Eclaireur

10, rue Hérold, 1st arr. (mixed inventory)
T: 10 40 41 09 89 • M: Sentier

12, rue Malher, 4th arr. (M)
T: 01 44 54 22 11 • M: Saint-Paul

3 ter, rue des Rosiers, 4th arr. (W)
T: 01 48 87 10 22 • M: Saint-Paul

26, avenue des Champs-Elysees, 8th arr. (M)
T: 01 45 62 12 32 • M: Franklin-D.-Roosevelt

Erotokritos

99, rue Vieille-du-Temple, 3rd arr.
T: 01 42 78 14 04 • M: Saint-Paul or Rambuteau

Fifi Chachnil

26, rue Cambon, 1st arr.
T: 01 42 60 38 86 • M: Concorde or Madeleine

231, rue Saint-Honoré, 1st arr.
T: 01 42 61 21 83 • M: Tuileries

Isabel Marant

1, rue Jacob, 6th arr.
T: 01 43 26 04 12 • M: Mabillon

Jamin Puech

68, rue Vieille-du-Temple, 3rd arr.
T: 01 48 87 84 87 • M: Saint-Paul
or Saint-Sébastien-Froissart

43, rue Madame, 6th arr.
T: 01 45 48 14 85 • M: Rennes or Saint-Placide

Judith Lacroix

61, rue Bonaparte, 6th arr.
T: 01 43 26 02 58 • M: Saint-Sulpice

Lacoste

37, bouelvard des Capucines, 2nd arr.
T: 01 42 61 58 20 • M: Opéra or Madeleine

28, Boulevard de Sébastopol, 4th arr.
T: 01 48 04 55 95 • RER: Les Halles

161, Boulevard Saint-Germain, 6th arr.
T: 01 53 63 25 00 • M: Saint-Germain-des-Prés

70-72, rue du Faubourg-Saint-Antoine, 12th arr.
T: 01 43 45 03 09 • M: Bastille or Ledru-Rollin

W: Women • M: Men • C: Children • B: Babies

53, avenue des Ternes, 17th arr.
T: 01 43 80 10 33 • M: Ternes
or Charles-de-Gaulle-Etoile

Maria Luisa

19 bis, rue du Mont-Thabor, 1st arr. (M)
T: 01 42 60 89 83 • M: Concorde or Tuileries

38, rue du Mont-Thabor, 1st arr. (mixed inventory)
T: 01 42 96 47 81 • M: Concorde

40, rue du Mont-Thabor, 1st arr. (mostly shoes)
T: 01 47 03 48 08 • M: Concorde

Maud Perl

39, rue de Grenelle, 7th arr.
T: 01 45 44 26 27 • M: Rue-du-Bac

Olga

45, rue de Turenne, 3rd arr.
T: 01 42 72 44 92 • M: Saint-Paul
or Chemin-Vert

103, rue Vieille-du-Temple, 3rd arr.
T: 01 42 71 16 93 • M: Fille-du-Calvaire or Saint-Sébastien-Froissart

Paul & Joe

46, rue Etienne-Marcel, 2nd arr.
(mixed inventory)
T: 01 40 28 03 34 • M: Séntier or Etienne-Marcel

40, rue du Four, 6th arr.
T: 01 45 44 97 70 • M: Saint-Sulpice

62, rue des Saint-Peres, 7th arr. (W)
T: 01 42 22 47 01 • M: Sevres-Babylone
or Saint-Sulpice

123, rue de la Pompe, 16th arr. (W)
T: 01 45 53 01 08 • M: Rue-de-la-Pompe

Vanessa Bruno

12, rue de Castiglione, 1st arr.
T: 01 42 61 44 60 • M: Tuileries

100, rue Vieille-du-Temple, 3rd arr.
T: 01 42 77 19 41 • M: Saint-Sébastien-Froissart

Ventilo

13-15, boulevard de la Madeleine, 1st arr.
T: 01 42 60 46 40 • M: Madeleine

10, rue des Francs-Bourgeois, 3rd arr.
T: 01 40 27 05 58 • M: Saint-Paul

59, rue Bonaparte, 6th arr.
T: 01 43 26 64 84 • M: Saint-Sulpice
or Saint-Germain-des-Prés

96, avenue Paul-Doumer, 16th arr.
T: 01 40 50 02 21 • M: La Muette

49, avenue Victor-Hugo, 16th arr.
T: 01 40 67 71 70 • M: Victor-Hugo

Zadig & Voltaire

9, rue du 29-Juillet, 1st arr. (W)
T: 01 42 92 00 80 • M: Tuileries

15, rue du Jour, 1st arr. (W, C)
T: 01 42 21 88 70 • RER: Les Halles

11, rue Monmartre, 1st arr. (M)
T: 10 40 13 00 54 • RER: Les Halles

42, rue des Francs-Bourgeois, 3rd arr. (W)
T: 01 44 54 00 60 • M: Saint-Paul
Outlet: 22, rue du Bourg-Tibourg, 4th arr.

T: 01 44 59 39 62 • M: Saint-Paul
or Hotel-de-Ville

16, rue Pavée, 4th arr. (M, W)
T: 01 44 59 39 06 • M: Saint-Paul

22, rue de Turenne, 4th arr. (W, M, C)
T: 01 42 71 81 12 • M: Saint-Paul

1, rue du Vieux-Colombier, 6th arr. (W, M, C)
T: 01 43 29 18 29 • M: Saint-Sulpice

3, rue du Vieux-Colombier, 6th arr. (W)
T: 01 45 48 39 37 • M: Saint-Sulpice

18-20, rue Francois-1er, 8th arr. (W, M, C)
T: 01 40 70 97 89 • M: Franklin-D.-Roosevelt

ALL SHOPS BY ARRONDISSEMENT

1ST ARRONDISSEMENT

* Agnès B. (page 12)
  6, rue du Jour, 1st arr.
  T: 01 45 08 56 56 • RER: Les Halles

  Agnès B.
  2, rue du Jour, 1st arr. (C)
  T: 01 40 39 96 88 • RER: Les Halles

  Agnès B.
  3, rue du Jour, 1st arr. (M)
  T: 01 42 33 04 13 • RER: Les Halles

  Agnès B.
  19, rue du Jour, 1st arr. (B)
  T: 01 42 33 27 34 • RER: Les Halles

* American Apparel (page 14)
  31, place du Marché-Saint-Honoré, 1st arr.
  T: 01 42 60 03 72 • M: Pyramides

* Antik Batik (page 16)
  4, rue Cambon, 1st arr.
  T: 01 40 15 01 45 • M: Concorde

* Chantal Thomass (page 20)
  211, rue Saint-Honoré, 1st arr.
  T: 01 42 60 40 56 • M: Tuileries

* Colette (page 23)
  213, rue Saint-Honoré, 1st arr.
  T: 01 55 35 33 90 • M: Tuileries

  L'Éclaireur
  10, rue Hérold, 1st arr. (mixed inventory)
  T: 10 40 41 09 89 • M: Sentier

  Fifi Chachnil
  231, rue Saint-Honoré, 1st arr.
  T: 01 42 61 21 83 • M: Tuileries

* Fifi Chachnil (page 26)
  68, rue Jean-Jacques-Rousseau, 1st arr.
  T: 01 42 21 19 93 • RER: Les Halles

  Fifi Chachnil
  26, rue Cambon, 1st arr.
  T: 01 42 60 38 86 • M: Concorde or Madeleine

* Gabrielle Geppert (page 30)
  31, galerie de Montpensier,

jardin du Palais-Royal, 1st arr.
T: 01 42 61 53 52

* Madame André (page 34)
  34, rue du Mont-Thabor, 1st arr.
  T: 01 42 96 27 24 • M: Concorde

* Maria Luisa (page 36)
  2, rue Cambon, 1st arr.
  T: 01 47 03 96 15 • M: Concorde

Maria Luisa
19 bis, rue du Mont-Thabor, 1st arr. (M)
T: 01 42 60 89 83 • M: Concorde or Tuileries

Maria Luisa
38, rue du Mont-Thabor, 1st arr.
(mixed inventory)
T: 01 42 96 47 81 • M: Concorde

Maria Luisa
40, rue du Mont-Thabor, 1st arr. (mostly shoes)
T: 01 47 03 48 08 • M: Concorde

* Michel Vivien (page 40)
  15, rue Molière, 1st arr.
  T: 01 42 96 38 20
  M: Palais-Royal-Musée-du-Louvre

* Le Mont Saint-Michel (page 42)
  29, rue du Jour, 1st arr.
  T: 01 53 40 80 44 • RER: Les Halles

* Pierre Hardy (page 44)
  156, galerie de Valois,
  jardin du Palais-Royal, 1st arr.
  T: 01 42 60 59 75
  M: Palais-Royal-Musée-du-Louvre

Vanessa Bruno
12, rue de Castiglione, 1st arr.
T: 01 42 61 44 60 • M: Tuileries

Ventilo
13-15, boulevard de la Madeleine, 1st arr.
T: 01 42 60 46 40 • M: Madeleine

* Veronique Leroy (page 46)
  10, rue d'Alger, 1st arr.
  T: 01 49 26 93 59 • M: Tuileries

Zadig & Voltaire
9, rue du 29-Juillet, 1st arr. (W)
T: 01 42 92 00 80 • M: Tuileries

Zadig & Voltaire
15, rue du Jour, 1st arr. (W, C)
T: 01 42 21 88 70 • RER: Les Halles

Zadig & Voltaire
11, rue Monmartre, 1st arr. (M)
T: 10 40 13 00 54 • RER: Les Halles

* indicates main listing
W: Women • M: Men • C: Children • B: Babies

2ND ARRONDISSEMENT

* Almost Famous (page 48)
  65, rue d'Argout, 2nd arr.
  T: 01 40 41 05 21 • M: Sentier

* Erotokritos (page 50)
  58, rue d'Argout, 2nd arr.
  T: 01 42 21 44 60 • M: Sentier

  Lacoste
  37, bouelvard des Capucines, 2nd arr.
  T: 01 42 61 58 20 • M: Opéra or Madeleine

  Paul & Joe
  46, rue Etienne-Marcel, 2nd arr.
  (mixed inventory)
  T: 01 40 28 03 34 • M: Séntier or Etienne-Marcel

* Repetto (page 53)
  22, rue de la Paix, 2nd arr.
  T: 01 44 71 83 12 • M: Opéra

* Ventilo (page 56)
  27 bis, rue du Louvre, 2nd arr.
  T: 01 44 76 82 97 • RER: Les Halles
  or M: Sentier

3RD ARRONDISSEMENT

* No 60 (page 60)
  60, rue Charlot, 3rd arr. (page TK)
  T: 01 44 78 91 90 • M: Filles-du-Calvaire

* AB 33 (page 60)
  33, rue Charlot, 3rd arr.
  T: 01 42 71 02 82 • M: Filles-du-Calvaire

  American Apparel
  123, rue Vieille-du-Temple, 3rd arr.
  T: 01 44 54 33 44
  M: Saint-Sébastien-Froissart

  A.P.C.
  112, rue Vieille-du-Temple, 3rd arr. (W, M, C)
  T: 01 42 78 18 02
  M: Saint-Sébastien-Froissart

* Les Belles Images (page 62)
  74, rue Charlot, 3rd arr.
  T: 01 42 76 93 61 • M: République
  or Filles-du-Calvaire

  Erotokritos
  99, rue Vieille-du-Temple, 3rd arr.
  T: 01 42 78 14 04 • M: Saint-Paul or Rambuteau

* Gaspard Yurkievich (page 66)
  43, rue Charlot, 3rd arr.
  T: 01 42 77 42 48 • M: Filles-du-Calvaire

* Hoses (page 69)
  41, rue de Poitou, 3rd arr.
  T: 01 42 78 80 62 • M: Filles-du-Calvaire
  or Saint-Sébastien-Froissart

Jamin Puech
  68, rue Vieille-du-Temple, 3rd arr.
  T: 01 48 87 84 87 • M: Saint-Paul
  or Sébastien-Froissart

* Martin Grant (page 72)
  10, rue Charlot, 3rd arr., Stair A, 2nd floor
  T: 01 42 71 39 49 • M: Saint-Sébastien-Froissart

Olga
  45, rue de Turenne, 3rd arr.
  T: 01 42 72 44 92 • M: Saint-Paul or Chemin-Vert

Olga
  103, rue Vieille-du-Temple, 3rd arr.
  T: 01 42 71 16 93 • M: Fille-du-Calvaire
  or Saint-Sébastien-Froissart

*RTA (page 78)
  3, rue Cunin-Gridaine, 3rd arr.
  T: 01 48 87 17 12 • M: Arts-et-Métiers

* Samy Chalon (page 80)
  24, rue Charlot, 3rd arr.
  T: 01 44 59 39 16 • M: Filles-du-Calvaire

* Shine (page 84)
  15, rue de Poitou, 3rd arr.
  T: 01 48 05 80 10 • M: Filles-du-Calvaire

* Studio W (page 86)
  6, rue du Pont-aux-Choux, 3rd arr.
  T: 01 44 78 05 02 or 06 10 66 14 66
  M: Saint-Sébastien-Froissart

* Tsumori Chisato (page 90)
  20, rue Barbette, 3rd arr.
  T: 01 42 78 18 88 • M: Saint-Paul

Vanessa Bruno
  100, rue Vieille-du-Temple, 3rd arr.
  T: 01 42 77 19 41
  M: Saint-Sébastien-Froissart

Ventilo
  10, rue des Francs-Bourgeois, 3rd arr.
  T: 01 40 27 05 58 • M: Saint-Paul

Zadig & Voltaire
  42, rue des Francs-Bourgeois, 3rd arr. (W)
  T: 01 44 54 00 60 • M: Saint-Paul

4TH ARRONDISSEMENT

American Apparel
  41, rue du Temple, 4th arr.
  T: 01 42 74 71 03 • M: Hotel-de-Ville

L'Eclaireur
12, rue Malher, 4th arr. (M)
T: 01 44 54 22 11 • M: Saint-Paul

L'Eclaireur
3 ter, rue des Rosiers, 4th arr. (W)
T: 01 48 87 10 22 • M: Saint-Paul

* Facteur Céleste (page 93)
38, rue Quincampoix, 4th arr.
T: 01 42 77 12 46 • M: Rambuteau
or RER: Les Halles

* Joy (page 96)
38, rue du Roi-de-Sicile, 4th arr.
T: 01 42 78 94 88 • M: Saint-Paul
or Hôtel-de-Ville

Lacoste
28, Boulevard de Sébastopol, 4th arr.
T: 01 48 04 55 95 • RER: Les Halles

* Maud Perl (page 100)
106, rue Vieille-du-Temple, 4th arr.
T: 01 42 71 30 87
M: Saint-Sébastien-Froissart

* Trésor by Brigitte Masson (page 102)
6, rue du Trésor, 4th arr.
T: 01 42 72 54 92 • M: Saint-Paul

Zadiq & Voltaire
Outlet: 22, rue du Bourg-Tibourg, 4th arr.
T: 01 44 59 39 62 • M: Saint-Paul
or Hotel-de-Ville

Zadiq & Voltaire
16, rue Pavée, 4th arr. (M, W)
T: 01 44 59 39 06 • M: Saint-Paul

Zadiq & Voltaire
22, rue de Turenne, 4th arr. (W, M, C)
T: 01 42 71 81 12 • M: Saint-Paul

6TH ARRONDISSEMENT

Agnès B.
83, rue d'Assas, 6th arr. (C)
T: 01 43 54 69 21 • M: Port-Royal

Agnès B.
13, rue Michelet, 6th arr. (W)
T: 01 46 33 70 20 • M: Port-Royal

Agnès B.
6, rue du Vieux-Colombier, 6th arr. (M)
T: 01 44 39 02 60 • M: Saint-Sulpice

Agnès B.
10-12, rue du Vieux-Colombier, 6th arr. (W)
T: 01 45 49 02 05 • M: Saint-Sulpice

American Apparel
7, rue Gozlin, 6th arr.
T: 01 40 46 02 00 • M: Saint-Germain-des-Prés

Antik Batik
20, rue Mabillon, 6th arr.
01 43 26 02 28 • M: Mabillon

A.P.C.
3, rue de Fleurus, 6th arr. (W)
T: 01 42 22 12 77 • M: Rennes or Saint-Placide

* A.P.C. (page 106)
4, rue de Fleurus, 6th arr. (mixed inventory)
T: 01 45 48 72 42 • M: Rennes or Saint-Placide

A.P.C.
Surplus: 45, rue Madame, 6th arr.
T: 01 45 48 43 71 • M: Rennes or Saint-Placide

* Dice Kayek (page 108)
10, rue du Cherche-Midi, 6th arr.
T: 01 42 22 51 05 • M: Saint-Sulpice

Isabel Marant
1, rue Jacob, 6th arr.
T: 01 43 26 04 12 • M: Mabillon

Jamin Puech
43, rue Madame, 6th arr.
T: 01 45 48 14 85 • M: Rennes or Saint-Placide

Judith Lacroix
61, rue Bonaparte, 6th arr.
T: 01 43 26 02 58 • M: Saint-Sulpice

* Kerstin Adolphson (page 111)
157, boulevard Saint-Germain, 6th arr.
T: 01 45 48 00 14 •
M: Saint-Germain-des-Prés

Lacoste
161, Boulevard Saint-Germain, 6th arr.
T: 01 53 63 25 00 •
M: Saint-Germain-des-Prés

Paul & Joe
40, rue du Four, 6th arr.
T: 01 45 44 97 70 • M: Saint-Sulpice

* Vanessa Bruno (page 114)
25, rue Saint-Sulpice, 6th arr.
T: 01 43 54 41 04 • M: Odéon or Mabillon

Ventilo
59, rue Bonaparte, 6th arr.
T: 01 43 26 64 84 • M: Saint-Sulpice
or Saint-Germain-des-Prés

Zadig & Voltaire
1, rue du Vieux-Colombier, 6th arr.
(W, M, C)
T: 01 43 29 18 29 • M: Saint-Sulpice

Zadiq & Voltaire
3, rue du Vieux-Colombier, 6th arr. (W)
T: 01 45 48 39 37 • M: Saint-Sulpice

7TH ARRONDISSEMENT

Maud Perl
39, rue de Grenelle, 7th arr.
T: 01 45 44 26 27 • M: Rue-du-Bac

Paul & Joe
62, rue des Saint-Peres, 7th arr. (W)
T: 01 42 22 47 01 • M: Sevres-Babylone
or Saint-Sulpice

* Les Prairies de Paris (page 118)
  6, rue du Pré-aux-Clercs, 7th arr
  T: 01 40 20 44 12 • M: Rue-du-Bac
  or Saint-Germain-des-Prés

Spree
1, rue de Saint-Simon, 7th arr.
T: 01 42 22 05 04 • M: Rue-du-Bac
or Solférino

8TH ARRONDISSEMENT

* L'Eclaireur (page 120)
  8, rue Boissy-d'Anglas, 8th arr.
  (mixed inventory)
  T: 01 53 43 03 70 • M: Concorde

L'Eclaireur
26, avenue des Champs-Elysees, 8th arr. (M)
T: 01 45 62 12 32 • M: Franklin-D.-Roosevelt

* Lacoste (page 124)
  93-95, avenue des Champs-Élysées, 8th arr.
  T: 01 47 23 39 26 • M: George-V

* Paul & Joe (page 128)
  2, avenue Montaigne, 8th arr.
  T: 01 47 20 57 50 • M: Alma-Marceau

Zadiq & Voltaire
18-20, rue Francois-1er, 8th arr. (W, M, C)
T: 01 40 70 97 89 • M: Franklin-D.-Roosevelt

9TH ARRONDISSEMENT

* Judith Lacroix (page 131)
  3, rue Henri-Monnier, 9th arr.
  T: 01 48 78 22 37 • M: Saint-Georges

* Karine Arabian (page 134)
  4, rue Papillon, 9th arr.
  T: 01 45 23 23 24 • M: Cadet or Poissonnière

* Mamie (page 138)
  73, rue de Rochechouart, 9th arr.
  T: 01 42 82 09 98 • M: Anvers

10TH ARRONDISSEMENT

Agnès B.
1, rue Dieu, 10th arr. (sportswear)
T: 01 42 03 47 99 • M: République

American Apparel
10, rue Beaurepaire, 10th arr.
T: 01 42 49 50 01 • M: République

* Jamin Puech (page 140)
61, rue d'Hauteville, 10th arr.
T: 01 40 22 08 32 • M: Poissonnière

11TH ARRONDISSEMENT

* Anne Willi (page 144)
13, rue Keller, 11th arr.
T: 01 48 06 74 06 • M: Ledru-Rollin

* French Trotters (page 146)
30, rue de Charonne, 11th arr.
T: 01 47 00 84 35 • M: Ledru-Rollin

* Gaëlle Barré (page 150)
17, rue Keller, 11th arr.
T: 01 43 14 63 02 • M: Ledru-Rollin

* Isabel Marant (page 152)
16, rue de Charonne, 11th arr.
T: 01 49 29 71 55 • M: Ledru-Rollin or Bastille

* Sessùn (page 156)
30, rue de Charonne, 11th arr.
T: 01 48 06 55 66 • M: Ledru-Rollin

12TH ARRONDISSEMENT

Agnès B.
Cour Saint-Emilion, wine storehouse No. 5,
12th arr. (mixed inventory)
T: 01 43 47 36 59 • M: Cour-Saint-Emilion

Lacoste
70-72, rue du Faubourg-Saint-Antoine,
12th arr.
T: 01 43 45 03 09 • M: Bastille
or Ledru-Rollin

* Louison (page 159)
20, rue Saint-Nicolas, 12th arr.
T: 01 43 44 02 62 • M: Ledru-Rollin

16TH ARRONDISSEMENT

Agnès B.
17, avenue pierre-1er-de-Serbie,
16th arr. (W)
T: 01 40 70 04 01 • M: Iéna

* Komplex (page 162)
118, rue de Longchamp, 16th arr.
T: 01 44 05 38 33 • M: Rue-de-la-Pompe

Paul & Joe
123, rue de la Pompe, 16th arr. (W)
T: 01 45 53 01 08 • M: Rue-de-la-Pompe

Ventilo
96, avenue Paul-Doumer, 16th arr.
T: 01 40 50 02 21 • M: La Muette

Ventilo
49, avenue Victor-Hugo, 16th arr.
T: 01 40 67 71 70 • M: Victor-Hugo

* **Zadiq & Voltaire** (page 165)
16 bis, rue de Passy, 16th arr.
T: 01 45 25 04 07 • M: Passy

17TH ARRONDISSEMENT

Lacoste
53, avenue des Ternes, 17th arr.
T: 01 43 80 10 33 • M: Ternes
or Charles-de-Gaulle-Etoile

18TH ARRONDISSEMENT

* **Série Limitee** (page 168)
20, rue Houdon, 18th arr.
T: 01 42 55 40 85 • M: Abbesses

* **Spree** (page 170)
16, rue La Vieuville, 18th arr.
T: 01 42 23 41 40 • M: Abbesses

INDEX

About the Author

Adrienne Ribes-Tiphaine has two passions, journalism and fashion. Born in 1973, after studying political sociology, she wrote for *Nova Magazine* under the direction of Jean-Francois Bizot. She has written for *Vogue France*, and is now a freelance writer for *ELLE*, *Atmosphere*, *Rendez-Vous*, and *France-Amerique*. In 2003, she published *Paris sur mesure* (Parigramme).

About the Photographer

Sandrine Alouf is a French photographer. She recently installed photographs of clouds along the platforms of the RER Luxembourg station in Paris in an exhibition called "A ciel ouvert" ('Open to the Skies").